The Legion in the Trenches

The Legion in the Trenches

Two Accounts of the French Foreign Legion
During the First World War

Kelly of the Foreign Legion

Russell A. Kelly

A Soldier of the Legion

Edward Morlae

LEONAUR

The Legion in the Trenches
Two Accounts of the French Foreign Legion During the First World War
Kelly of the Foreign Legion
by Russell A. Kelly
and
A Soldier of the Legion
by Edward Morlae

First published under the titles
Kelly of the Foreign Legion
and
A Soldier of the Legion

Leonaur is an imprint
of Oakpast Ltd

ISBN: 978-0-85706-962-7 (hardcover)
ISBN: 978-0-85706-963-4 (softcover)

http://www.leonaur.com

Publisher's Notes

The views expressed in this book are not necessarily
those of the publisher.

Contents

Kelly of the Foreign Legion

Contents

DEDICATED TO THE MEMORY
OF THAT INTREPID AND VALIANT FRENCHMAN,
WHOSE BRAVERY, LOVE OF LIBERTY,
GENEROSITY, AND FRIENDSHIP
WITH WASHINGTON,
MADE AMERICANS, FOR ALL TIME,
HIS GRATEFUL AND DEVOTED ADMIRERS—
LE MARQUIS DE LAFAYETTE

Preface

The first seven chapters of this book are letters received from Russell A. Kelly, age 21, volunteer in the *Légion étrangère*. The letters, many of which were published in the *New York Evening Sun*, were sent to his parents in New York and have been retained in exactly their original form except for the omission of strictly personal matters.

The last communication from him was a military post card mailed June, 15th, 1915. After the severe engagement around Souchez on June 16th in which the Second *Regiment de Marche* of the First Regiment of the Legion suffered severely, he was officially recorded by the French Minister of War as "missing," with the added statement that his name would be carried on the list of missing until a search could be made in the internment camps of Germany.

Exhaustive efforts have been made to locate him. All information that has been obtained as to his fate is given in Chapter 9.

When it was learned in New York that he had enlisted, he was informed that Germany had, prior to the war, objected to the Foreign Legion as a military body, and had stated that *Légionnaires* who were not French citizens would be considered as non-combatants and not entitled to the rights of the other soldiers of the French army.

He was accordingly advised that in the event of his capture to give no information as to his citizenship; but to communicate with Ambassador Gerard. He answered that he would follow those instructions.

Chapter 2534 of the laws passed by Congress March 2nd, 1907, makes the taking of an oath of allegiance to a foreign king or state an act of expatriation for an American citizen.

But as Russell did not and was not required to take an oath of allegiance to France, he continued, after enlistment, to be a citizen of the United States of America.

Acknowledgment is made to the *New York Evening Sun* for permission to print those letters which appeared in that paper.

J. E. K.

New York. May, 1917.

CHAPTER 1

Voyage to Bordeaux—Enlistment

Bordeaux, France,
36 Rue Notre Dame,
Wednesday, Nov. 25, 1914.

On Election Day, Tuesday November 3rd, 1914, we left New York, from the South Brooklyn basin, on "the good ship" *Orcadian* with a cargo of six hundred and fifty horses for the use of the French army. There were twenty-five men, including my chum Larney and myself, who had not previously worked on ships nor around horses, and eight experienced horsemen. We twenty-five consisted of twelve Englishmen, seven Italians, two Greeks, one Spaniard, and three Americans, the third being a negro. The first day the ship was out the English and Italians started to fight, and this divided the party into two messes; at every meal thereafter there were hostilities. The third day out we ran into very rough weather, which continued during the following day: the vessel rolled and pitched in a horrible fashion, and most of us suffered severely from sea sickness.

The food furnished to us was very poor. The first nine meals consisted of Irish stew, and I believe it was made on the first day and thereafter heated at meal time.

We went *en masse* to the chief steward and demanded better food; there was a change, but it was no better, it was only different.

The horses were fed twice a day, the first time in the morning from half-past five to eight o'clock. We then had breakfast followed by hoisting feed from the hold, cleaning the stalls and similar duties, and then dinner. At three in the afternoon we gave the horses their second feeding, which took until nearly six o'clock when we had supper.

In rough weather life on the boat was fierce. Watering the horses as the boat rolled usually resulted in much of the water getting on the men, and the deck was always wet and slippery.

A cabin meant to hold twelve seamen held thirty-three cattlemen, so conditions can be realized. The air was foul; in fact the whole ship was foul. During the last week I slept in the lowest deck on the hay. We could not eat the food furnished, and even had it been palatable, it lacked quantity, so my appetite was not appeased once during the trip. I lost about fifteen pounds during the voyage. I could wash only twice and shave once during the trip. English warships convoyed us for the entire voyage, yet there was much uneasiness among the men. We lost eighteen horses *en route*.

On November 19th we were in that part of the Atlantic called the Bay of Biscay, and entering the broad Gironde River proceeded up it for about thirty miles to Pauillac, off which we laid two days, and then went up the river another thirty miles to Bordeaux where we docked at seven in the morning of Saturday November 21st. It was snowing and the city did not seem real—it looked so quaint and picturesque.

At ten o'clock we were dressed and went ashore and were stopped on the wharf by a Customs official who looked in only one valise and that was for tobacco and matches. The party then proceeded to a wine shop, where some bought wine, that they said was good, for fifteen *centimes* a glass. We soon learned that this was only three cents of American money.

We left our hand baggage at this shop and went to the British consul, from whom we received our discharge. We then returned for the bags and sought lodgings, which we obtained on Rue Notre Dame.

Everything we see in the city is different from anything my chum Larney or I have seen in America: the sidewalks and roadways are very narrow; the buildings quaint in appearance and generally only two stories in height.

We had a good supper although the portions served were small, but, as is usual, they gave three kinds of meat at the meal. Coffee was served in a small bowl with heated milk, there being more milk than coffee. For dessert nuts were served. The rooms were without heat, and for light a small torch was used.

On Sunday Larney and I with the two Greeks from the ship, went around town, one of the Greeks being the only member who could speak French.

Monday morning the four of us found the station for recruiting for the army and made application to join the Foreign Legion. The officers were agreeable but evinced no desire to urge us to enlist, and they informed us of an old rule in the Legion, that an applicant will not be examined or accepted until the day following his application. So we returned Tuesday morning at eight o'clock and took the physical examination, which was very thorough and the four of us were accepted.

Twenty other men who meant to join the regular army were examined at the same time, six of whom were rejected, some solely on account of poor teeth.

At five o'clock in the afternoon of Tuesday, November 24th, 1914, we signed articles which made us soldiers in the Army of the Republic of France, in the division *la Légion étrangère*, for service during the war.

We were not asked to take any oath of allegiance to France, nor to renounce our allegiance to the United States; all that was required of us was to be over eighteen years of age and to pass the doctor.

We were given five *francs* (one dollar) as spending money, and a railroad ticket to Lyon, where one of the depots of the Foreign Legion is located. It is to be our training station for four or five months, they say, before we can go to the front. No escort was furnished or effort made to see that we reported at Lyon and we learned it was the custom even before the war to trust recruits for the Legion to reach the depot of their own accord. We had time to take a further look around Bordeaux. We met soldiers in large numbers everywhere, and found they were of the same belief as the people generally—that the Germans would be defeated in two months. All theatres were closed except some moving picture shows, the receipts from them were given to the Red Cross fund.

Lyon,
December 2, 1914.

We left Bordeaux Wednesday night at nine o'clock, riding second class. The cars are small and divided into compartments, each holding eight persons. Most of the passengers were soldiers returning to the front. It was difficult to sleep as the train stopped every half hour and the people getting off and on made considerable noise.

Thursday was a clear day, and the bright sunlight enabled us to enjoy the magnificent scenery. The train was climbing mountains and going at a moderate pace. The construction of this railroad was a great engineering feat. One minute we would be in a tunnel, then suddenly emerge onto a frail bridge over a magnificent valley.

Nearly all the land in sight was under cultivation, it being divided into small plots of about half an acre each. These plots were enclosed by stone walls three feet high and two feet thick and the walls extended as far as the eye could see. The people were all very friendly but the only one of our party who could talk to them was our Greek interpreter.

From our hotel in Bordeaux we brought a roast chicken, bread and wine, which we ate at noon. The people here roast a chicken with its head on. We took the wine not because we were wine drinkers, but because the landlord put it in as a regular part of every lunch.

This is a great country for churches; from the car window we saw many that were nearly as imposing as cathedrals, and some had only ten or fifteen cottages around them.

We arrived at Lyon at one in the afternoon and went direct to the depot or station of the Legion.

We were temporarily assigned to the Fifth company of the Premier or First regiment. Our barrack was a school house before the war. We were located in a room about twenty feet wide and of the same length, the ceiling being about ten feet high. Maps and cards were still on the walls, and the desks and benches were piled in a comer.

When we arrived there were eight men in the room and newcomers continued to come until we had twenty-five men in the room. Each man was given a straw mattress, a pillow and two blankets.

We found nearly every nationality represented in this Foreign Legion; there were, however, no Chinese nor Japanese.

They have a system, when furnishing the men's outfit, that enables a man to realize some money. Each man is given a complete outfit but should he have some articles of clothing that could be substituted for the military ones he is allowed a fair price for them and does not get equivalent articles from the quartermaster. For example, I had two winter union suits and a heavy sweater for which I received seventeen *francs* (three dollars and thirty-five cents) and got no underclothes from the army. One man received ninety *francs* (seventeen dollars and a half) that way.

We got a complete outfit and Larney and I had our pictures taken. I enclose one of mine.

By looking closely at the cap in the picture it will be seen that it has a cover on it. The cap is made of red cloth, but that colour being too conspicuous a blue linen cover is worn over it. The coat is blue and reaches to the knees; it is buttoned back to allow free movement. The trousers are bright red, but were found to be such a good target at the beginning of the war, that a sort of blue overall is issued at the front to hide the red trousers. Patent leather *puttees* are generally worn, but in this photo I wear Douglas shoes. The regulation ones are very heavy; by actual count each shoe has one hundred and sixty-two hobs in the sole, which is half an inch thick. I never thought I would put my feet into things like them, much less wear them.

A broad band will be noticed around my waist. This is of blue linen and is fifteen feet long. It is the positive insignia of our Legion, and is not worn by any other division of the French army. A broad leather belt with a brass buckle supports the bayonet, the hilt of which is visible at my left side. This is a murderous weapon, and I do not blame the Germans for being afraid of it. It is about a foot and nine inches long and comes to a needle point. It has four grooves, and each edge is a quarter inch deep and one-eighth inch wide at the hilt. It is half an inch in diameter at the hilt. The gun has an eight shell chamber and one shell in the barrel; it is six inches longer than the present U. S. army gun.

With bayonet attached it is a formidable weapon. This is our dress uniform, the one we appear in when on the street. The fatigue uniform has a cap or *beret* which is comfortable and handy, a short blouse, dark blue, no coat, the same pants and *puttees*. The blue band insignia we always wear.

CHAPTER 2

Training at Depot de Lyon

Lyon,
December 12, 1914.

Reveille sounds at half-past five in the morning; we are then served with coffee, followed by drill till half-past ten when we have dinner, consisting of rich soup, meat, potatoes, etc. We get no sweets whatsoever. After dinner we peel potatoes, and after that drill till half-past four, at which time we have supper, there being the same bill of fare as dinner. We are free from five-thirty until nine, when we have inspection and then sleep. It is hard to get accustomed to the drill as the commands are in French, and scarcely any of the soldiers understand that language, even slightly. Last Sunday we walked through the city in the company of an Englishman who came from Ceylon to enlist. He is a "younger son" and spends money lavishly when he has it. At present he is not in funds.

To the east of Lyon is a range of mountains, and on one of the highest mountains is a church. We visited it while military service was being held and the edifice was crowded. It has the handsomest and most costly interior decorations of any church I have ever seen. It is called the Chapelle de Notre Dame de Fourvière.

The view from the heights was magnificent. Lyon is in a valley and has two rivers running through it very swiftly. They say that Mt. Blanc, in Switzerland, can be seen from this church on a clear day. We saw many snow-capped mountains in the distance, but as the day was overcast we could not see the main attraction.

Last Monday we were transferred to the 2nd company of the

same First *Régiment étrangère.* This is to be our permanent company and it is in another barracks. The day before we reached Lyon two Americans arrived from La Rochelle where they had enlisted. One had seen service in the Philippines, in the cavalry, while the other had served in the navy. So we were not so lonely after all.

When we reached the new barracks we found four more Americans, one of whom had been in the army, another in the navy; one was a doctor and the other a lawyer. The doctor is forty-nine years old; he came over at the beginning of the war to join the Red Cross. The ex-army man fought in the insurrection in Chili, and served in Mexico under Villa and he works a machine gun. He has since left us for the front.

These new barracks are located in a new school house, not quite completed. Our room is about ninety feet long and thirty feet wide; it has a row of eight windows on each side, and accommodates one hundred men.

At intervals of about a week volunteers who desire to go to the front are called for from the different companies. Of course we volunteered, but were refused because there is a severe form of typhoid in the trenches which, it is said, kills a man in four hours. On this account nobody is allowed to go until he has been inoculated four times; we had not been inoculated at all. The volunteers are put in a special company and drilled separately. Larney and I with the three other Americans (the doctor not included) are in this company.

This Legion is the most cosmopolitan organisation in the world. In one corner of the room you will hear Greek spoken, the next group will be speaking Spanish, then German spdken by the Swiss, Polish from another corner and English from our crowd.

I saw a fight through interpreters. A Greek got into an unintelligible argument with a Pole and as neither could speak the other's language nor *"parly"* French, their fellow countrymen were called, and they being slightly acquainted with French, that was the language resorted to. When all arrangements were completed the combatants proceeded to pommel each other, and before long the interpreters were also engaged, and it was a very lively party when the officers arrived. There are many such happenings and they afford much amusement.

21

We have had many sham battles and considerable rifle practice. I now, five weeks after reaching barracks, make an average of four hits out of eight at a target of a man, life size, at two hundred and fifty metres (298 yards). They call that fair shooting for the time in practice.

The manual of arms is very different from that of the Virginia Military Institute, but the training I received there comes in handy. I cannot understand the commands but generally know what to expect.

All the men in our section have the same limited knowledge of French, but they are able to understand the orders. The weather is warm; an overcoat is only necessary at night.

Lyon,
January 17, 1916.

I miss sweets very much. Many times I have longed for a piece of pie, in fact for a whole pie, but they do not know what pie is over here. The pastry in the shops is wonderfully light but ridiculously expensive, and our pay of one cent a day does not permit investing in it. Still we have indulged several times, but it seemed like eating samples. I certainly miss the sweets.

I also missed the Thanksgiving Day dinner; we had nothing extra that day, so while eating mine I thought of the folks at home and the good things they were enjoying. But I missed the Christmas dinner most; we received no extra course here, so I contented myself with philosophizing, and speculating on the next Christmas dinner. Larney said he will have his in Berlin, but I prefer mine at *home*.

We had the first fall of snow in Lyon this morning. It lasted about two minutes. Instead of cold and snow they have a rainy winter. There have not been two successive days without showers since I arrived in France.

Trolley cars, with overhead wires, are used in Lyon and they are run with a trailer. There are many kinds; some are divided into three compartments, one-third of the car being devoted to standing room, and the other two divisions being for first and second classes. I have seen a car pass with the second class packed as closely as they are in the New York Subway, while the first class was empty. The first class fare is double that of the second.

The ear is started by a signal from a small horn, and the conductor gives a receipt as he collects the fare. Double deck trolleys have been in use here for years.

I tried to learn the location at the front of the First *Régiment étrangère*, but nobody knows. There were six Americans here and two have left for the front. We received letters from them but they were not allowed to give their location and the envelopes had a number in place of the name of the post office. Post offices near the front axe no longer named; they are numbered, and not in consecutive order, for *Secteur Postal 6* adjoins 109. Soldier's letters are sent free in France. Letters of prisoners of war are forwarded free (when they are forwarded) through all countries, including the neutrals who are in the postal union.

We learned that it is very cold where the First Regiment is and that an Italian who left here with the two Americans was given eight days in prison for eating his reserve rations.

A shipment of volunteers from our company left for the front three weeks ago and last week we were assembled and a report read stating that one of the men (giving his name) was executed, having been caught in the act of deserting. Considering these incidents, they must be near the front.

We called at the American Consulate and found the vice consul in charge. He had served in the Philippines during the war. He gave us New York newspapers and treated us with great kindness. While there an American doctor came in, who was disgusted with travelling facilities. His passport had his photograph attached. The paper was nearly covered with official stamps and he came to the Consul to get the U. S. stamp on while there was still room, as every Tom, Dick and Harry, he said, was desirous of spoiling the paper. When he saw Larney and I and learned we were from New York he became enthusiastic and gave ten *francs* to each of us. Another American gentleman and his wife came to the barracks one evening with the vice consul, and presented each of us with a package containing pipe, cigarettes, tobacco and a neck wrapper. We fully appreciated their acts. The gentleman had given his auto to the Red Cross and he drives it.

Great changes are taking place here. All the Legionaries who did not want to fight the Germans were shipped to Algiers. Another call for volunteers was made to all the companies. Those who did not volunteer were sent to Valbonne, a town about twenty miles off. There are a great many men there and they will remain, it is reported, until spring.

We cannot find out when we leave for the front, but all of us hope that it will be soon.

On December 31st I was inoculated for the third time against typhoid; it was the most severe of the four inoculations. We were treated at three p. m. and two hours after I thought I would die. I was sick all of the next day; at first I was troubled by a severe headache, followed by chills and fever. The fourth and last inoculation had no effect at all.

It may be interesting to describe how they inoculate. First the doctor, who is called in French, *le médecin*, asks you about the condition of your throat, chest and bowels. If they are O. K. he takes the flesh on the shoulder blade (he used my left four times, the right he rarely uses, and only then toward the finish) between the thumb and forefinger of his left hand, making a ridge of the flesh. The hypodermic needle is forced into the flesh and it felt to me as though it was pushed just under the skin. The fluid is then injected; it leaves a small lump on the blade until it begins to work on the system. The quantity of serum is gradually increased from the first treatment; I should judge the first time about a tablespoonful was used. Thank Heaven it is over. I am ready to leave at a moment's notice now.

Larney likes the life. He was issued a good overcoat, but was made to exchange it with a man going to the front. He did not like the first overcoat but was in raptures over the exchange.

When we first reached Lyon the city was alive with soldiers and it was surprising to note the great number of different uniforms the French army has. Of late, however, the diminishing number of soldiers on the streets is apparent. Most of the men were sent to Valbonne or the front.

Everybody in Lyon seems to be working for the army. Contracts are given to individual families for uniforms and wherever you go women and men are seen carrying military clothing for the soldiers, while wagons loaded with army clothes are very numerous.

All automobile works and machine shops, even the smallest, are busily engaged manufacturing shells and the arsenals are working two shifts of men, one night and one day.

It seems to me that our army is feeling a growing scarcity of rifles, as they are now issuing to recruits an old model rifle of fifty calibre. It is a single shot affair of 1867 model; rather awkward and crude. I have seen large motor trucks returning from the front laden down with rifles picked up from the battle fields. After an overhauling the guns will be used again.

I am struck very forcibly with the great economy of the French. We did fatigue the other day and it consisted of washing or rather scrubbing with brush and water the shoes returned from the front. I believe the bodies are stripped of what can be used again.

Wood is scarce over here; it must cost more than concrete. Concrete workers are very expert and some finishing work I saw by them was remarkable. These workmen, however, would be useless in the States, as it takes them too long to construct a building.

Everything is saved to the smallest item: even pig skins are saved to grease with. They are sold tied up in neat little rolls, and, I believe, sold by weight. Everything is sold by weight, even bread, which is excellent; no bread in the States can equal it.

Last Sunday while we were walking along the street a Frenchman stopped and talked to us in English. He had spent seven years in London. He was very pleasant and treated us royally and escorted us back to barracks. He invited us to call on him. A party of four of us, three Americans and a Spaniard, a few nights ago had a night march, with manoeuvres to take a fort. The sergeant in command was a Frenchman with no knowledge of any language except the French, so he had great difficulty in explaining the tactics to us. When we returned to barracks we were given hot wine flavoured with lemon; it was good. Tomorrow morning we start at three o'clock for a long hike. They believe in work here.

Lyon,
January 23, 1915.

We continue drilling hard; had a twenty-five mile hike the other day. Started at half-past six in the morning and returned at six in the afternoon. We cooked our dinner and it certainly was fine. We had wine, meat, fried potatoes, cheese, bread and coffee. If we get such meals at the front we will be well satisfied.

We are having night marches frequently, and always get hot wine when we return.

Our section was put on fire duty Sunday afternoon. At this duty we simply stack arms in the courtyard and wait around. In case of a fire in the city we are to keep the crowd hack. I think the main object of fire duty is to keep the men in barracks.

When we arrived in Lyon I purchased an English-French grammar but have had very little time to study and the light in the barracks at night is too poor to read by. But I will do the best I can to learn as much French as possible.

The censor does not seem to interfere with our mail; none of the letters I received has been tampered with.

We get all newspapers, magazines and other printed matter, without any attempt by the censor to examine them.

Our squad contains sixteen men and is divided into two rooms. In my room are two Americans (the Greek-American sailor is with me), two Italians, one German-Swiss, who is an excellent soldier, two Spaniards and an Arab. One of the Spaniards has been in prison twice and is now serving his third term, fifteen days this time. One of the Italians is a good soldier; the other is guilty of an unpardonable sin, he snores. He wakes us every night; last night the sailor threw a shoe at him; when it struck him he woke with a jump, and was going to take the sailor's life, but his music (?) had so provoked us that we were only waiting for an excuse to rend him limb from limb, so he wisely got under the covers. All in all we have a pretty good room.

It is comical when it comes to conversation. One day we talk English, the next Spanish, the next Italian, but we all agree Divine Wisdom was absent when the Arabic language was constructed. When an Arab talks it sounds as though he was choking to death. The language consists of spits and coughs, and at regular intervals a sneeze is employed to give the proper accent.

Larney is in the next room with John Smith (the fourth American), three Spaniards, a Swiss corporal, a Russian and a Greek. These three Spaniards are brothers and inseparable; the youngest is about thirty-five years old. They came from Argentina, having served in the artillery there; they are three excellent men. They were sent by the French consul at Argentina.

One of the Greeks who came over on the steamer with us and

enlisted at Bordeaux, has been reformed today, January 26th, and sent back to Bordeaux as he has consumption. This news completely nonplussed me as at the physical examination he showed up the best of us. He was well muscled and looked the picture of a trained athlete. He intends to go to Cape Town, South Africa, where he has a relative. He is a good-hearted chap and I am sorry for him.

Lyon,
January 30, 1915.

The number of Legionnaries training in Lyon has been steadily diminished until only one hundred remain. There are a great many Frenchmen, however, training in Lyon. At Valbonne, twenty miles from here, there we about thirty thousand troops training, among them several companies of the Legion.

Nearly all the public buildings are used as hospitals, while the schools have been converted into barracks.

The people are very pleasant and will go a great distance out of their way to set a stranger in the right direction. They are light eaters; bread, wine and cheese are their mainstays. A large amount of chocolate is eaten; it is not as good as our milk chocolate.

The moving picture shows in Lyon are free for soldiers. The people like the western cowboy pieces, I saw a string of six push-carts with advertisements of films in which John Bunny appeared.

We are paid one *sou*, being the equivalent of one cent, a day and pay-day every tenth day. Our dissipation on half a *franc* can be readily pictured. But we are furnished everything we need, and there are no charges here.

Market days are Tuesdays and Fridays, and on those days most of the public squares are thrown open to the farmers who come to town with long, narrow, two-wheeled carts, drawn by everything from a dog to a horse. Small donkeys, about three feet high, are numerous. One frequently sees a dog harnessed with a donkey; I saw an old woman teamed with a dog drawing a fruit cart. There are some fine draught horses; the animals work tandem, and the driver walks.

Four-wheeled carts are very scarce. Auto-trucks are used for transportation; many are of the large, heavy type, but have steel tires. Pleasure cars are numerous. The majority have been taken for military purposes. They are all built low and make considerable noise.

I have not as yet seen many asphalt covered streets. Most of them are paved with stone blocks, while in a great number of streets cobble stones are used. Save in the main streets, the sidewalks are narrow. As a rule the streets are well lighted at night. A great many places of business have signs "English spoken," but we have not yet come across one store wherein English was spoken. The stores are open on Sundays. Monday is the poorest business day in the week.

The children have school, if soldiers are not using the building, from nine to noon, and from two to four p. m. School is in session Saturdays but closed Thursdays.

Cette carte doit être remise au vaguemestre. RIEN ne doit y être ajouté, excepté la date et la signature de l'expéditeur; les phrases inutiles peuvent être biffées. *Si quelque chose y était ajouté, cette carte ne serait pas transmise.*

Je vais bien.

Je suis à l'hôpital { blessé } et suis en voie de guérison.
                   { malade } et j'espère être bientôt rétabli.

J'ai reçu votre { lettre.
                 { télégramme.
                 { paquet.

Je n'ai reçu aucune nouvelle de vous { dernièrement.
                                      { depuis longtemps.

Lettre suit à la première occasion.

Date (*sans indication d'origine*) _____

Lyon 2/5/15
                              Signature (seulement) :
Dear Dad :- We leave for the front
early to-morrow morning. We
have a complete outfit even to
the blue overalls over the red
pants. The colonel inspected us &
we passed this afternoon. It is
almost like summer now but it
can't last. Have written mother Russ

OFFICIAL POSTCARD FOR USE OF SOLDIERS

CHAPTER 3

Off to the Front

Lyon,
February 6, 1915.

At last the order we have so anxiously awaited has come; we leave early tomorrow morning, February 6th, for the front. We were given a complete outfit, which consisted of one suit of underclothes, two pairs of socks, a white cotton sleeping hat, two pairs of shoes, a neck muffler and a jacket which resembles a smoking jacket. These jackets are all the same size, which is small, so that a big fellow has a hard time getting into one. There is no warmth in them, so most of the fellows did not bother to pack them. I left mine with the underclothes in Lyon, not having room in the sack for them. We got blue overalls to go over the red pants. We also got a pair of mittens, but they are not much good.

We were given a loaf of bread, one can of sardines, one and a half cans of fish paste, a chunk of cheese and some chocolate for rations. As a reserve ration we got two cans of bully beef, hard tack, salt, pepper, tea, coffee and sugar.

We also got one hundred and twenty rounds of ammunition. We packed a blanket, and half of a shelter tent with poles. The complete pack weighed nearly seventy pounds; it was very heavy.

The colonel inspected us thoroughly, and we passed after close scrutiny.

The weather is mild and like summer.

31

Somewhere in France,
February 14, 1915.

We left barracks Saturday morning, February 6th, in a pouring rain, and our train left Lyon at ten o'clock.

We arrived at Noisy-le-Sec, which is on the eastern outskirts of Paris and about two hundred miles north of Lyon, at ten o'clock Sunday morning. We remained until ten o'clock in the evening and then proceeded to our railroad destination which was about seventy miles to the northeast of Paris, and from there we had about twenty *kilometres* (twelve and a half miles) to march to this town where we are now located.

Before reaching Noisy-le-Sec we passed a trainload of soldiers from India. It was a husky outfit.

There was a complete company of us, about two hundred and fifty. When we reached here our section was located in the loft of a barn. It was cold in our quarters as we had no stove and the weather was cold and rainy.

Upon reaching this place, the reserve rations given to us at Lyons were collected.

We are all well, and well treated and fed. We have coffee three times a day; wine once.

We were divided according to nationalities. Our section contained, besides Americans, Belgians, Swedes, Roumanians, Italians, English and a pure-blooded Egyptian, who is very dark.

This town is the quaintest place I have seen; it has no sidewalks, and there was no idea of regularity when it was laid out. There are only about six stores, and I should judge the place contains about three hundred people. The butcher comes through here twice a week with his stock of trade in a wagon. The principal industry around here is grape growing; farming is a side issue.

A short distance from the railroad station there is a small river very near the canal. Over the canal were once two bridges now both destroyed, so we marched over temporary ones. This was the first sign of destruction I have seen since I reached France. They say the French destroyed these bridges.

We drill here and the colonel manoeuvred us the other day; he was well satisfied with us. There is a high mountain range between us and the firing line and from sunrise until night we can hear the rumble of cannon; it sounds like distant thunder.

The two Americans who left us in Lyon have spent three weeks in the trenches. We met them here during their rest which tests eight days. They have returned to the trenches. The loss of life in the trenches has been reduced to a minimum. There is a constant rifle and cannon fire, but little damage is done while the men remain in the trenches.

I miss all of my folks and often think of New York. I am carrying a talisman in the form of a Yale key which belongs to the front door of our apartment. I have become attached to it and would feel its loss keenly. On the brace supporting the teeth is the word "Security." A person with a lively imagination might find some hidden meaning in this.

Our sailor Pavelka formerly entertained us every night with tales of his trip on the good ship *Dirigo* from Seattle to England *via* Cape Horn. Jack London made the same voyage on its previous trip. It took our sailor one hundred and fifty-nine days to make the trip. After supper when stories are being exchanged he usually starts with, "Now, fellows, when I was on the *Dirigo* off——" He only gets that far now, because, like most sailors, he is very voluble and his tales of the sea have become monotonous. However, we are a very congenial *quartette* and get along well together.

Dad says he has a complete map of France, giving small villages, but we are not allowed to tell our location.

Dad was always good at puzzles: does he remember this one?[1]

Boston ⎫
Orleans ⎪
Utopia ⎬ Does he get me?
Zion ⎪
Yapank ⎭

We take long marches. The roads are excellent and have a complete system of direction signs. Just after we started on one of these bikes I saw a sign reading "Rheims 24 *Kilometres*." As a *kilometre* is five-eighths of a mile, this was the equivalent of fifteen miles.

Somewhere in France (Bouzy),
February 28, 1915.

Things are about the same here; the weather is mild and we are having less rain. Ploughing is almost finished and planting

---

1. The name of the place indicated by this puzzle is Bouzy

33

will soon begin. From the outskirts of this place to the summit of the mountain (about three miles) the ground rises in a gentle slope which is completely covered by vineyards. It is a great wine country and from the heights a wonderful view is obtained of this extensive and fertile valley.

If Mr. Shortt's son is anxious to join the war, he can do so easily. I would advise him to hurry up; by that I do not mean that the war will soon be over; I know absolutely nothing about that. If he is not ready to secure passage immediately, he can slip over on a horse boat, as I learn they are still importing horses.

It is a matter of choice which regiment he joins, the First or Second. The Second contains the most Americans and it recruits through Paris; my regiment recruits through the southern ports,

I would strongly advise him to lose no time, but sail immediately. It makes no difference whether he knows French or not. I have often told you of the great percentage here who do not know the language. Let him bring as much money as he cares to, because one cannot do or see much on the salary they pay here of one cent a day. Former military training is not necessary, but on the other hand if he has any glaring physical defects, he will not be accepted. I was surprised at the rigidity with which the examination was conducted.

He should bring two suits of good woollen underclothes and about half a dozen pairs of thick woollen socks. If he is going to bring a shaving set it should be as small and compact as possible. His comb and brush should be small and he should bring a small mirror. He should not bring many other clothes as they will be useless when he gets into a uniform. The army does not furnish a storeroom, so I put mine in the Municipal Pawn Shop in Lyon. They allow a very small loan, but it is conducted by the government and is used by many for storage of silver and other valuables. Would advise him to bring a tooth brush in some kind of a stiff cover to protect the bristles.

Above all, impress him that he is not going to be a tourist. He carries everything on his back and believe me, after an entire day of hiking, every ounce counts. The complete pack with cartridges, rations, etc., weighs nearly seventy pounds, so there is absolutely no room for junk. I would advise him to bring some sort of a leather portfolio (not too big) to fit into his inside coat pocket to carry personal papers, etc. He need not worry about his outfit of clothes; the army attends to that. Show him in a philosophical way that he had better come. He has a leave from college, so he cannot lose anything by coming. On the other hand he will gain a lot of knowledge of the country, etc., and at his age it should almost be compulsory. I tell you candidly, if I was in his shoes I would get over here if I had to ship on a cattle boat. Well, here's luck to him and I hope to see him soon.[2]

Somewhere in France (Bouzy),
March 4. 1915.

I received the army hand-book today. These books are given to each soldier and contain an identification, list of crimes, penalties, etc., and information about the bearer. In case anything should happen to me, I give the following information from the book. It will simplify the searching of my records.

RUSSELL KELLY

		ETAT CIVIL		
Né le—13 Juin 1893.				
á- New York.				
Canton d- " "			Signalement.	
Départément d- New			Cheveux-	Blonde.
York.			Yeux-	gris bleu.
Residant á- Bordeaux.			Front-	
Départément d- Gironde.			Nez-	rectiligne.
Profession d- Sans.			Visage-	ovale.
Fils de-			Poids-	60 Kilos.
et de-			Taille- 1 mtr-75 cen-	
Domicilies á- Sans.			timetres.	
Canton d- "				
Départément d- "				

Ou Engagé, Volontaire; durée guerre, le 24 n'bre 1914,

á Bordeaux, département de Gironde.

Numéro de la Liste Matricule-997.

---

2. The young man referred to is Allan Shortt, son of Hon. William Allaire Shortt of Staten Island, New York. He subsequently joined the Fifty-Ninth Battalion, Canadians, was attached to the machine gun section, and became a lieutenant. He was missing following an engagement December 10th, 1916, on the front in France: he is now a prisoner.

RUSSELL KELLY.

Born the 13 June 1893.
at   New York.
County of   "   "
Department of New York.
Resident at Bordeaux.
Department of Gironde.
Profession of—without.
Son of
and of
Dwelling at, without.
County of   "
Department of "

SOCIAL STATE.

Description.

Hair	Blonde
Eyes	gray-blue
Forehead	
Nose	straight
Face	oval
Weight	132½ pounds
Height	5 feet 9 inches

Where engaged; volunteer; duration of the war, 24 November 1914, at Bordeaux, department of Gironde. Number on recruiting list—997.

A small aluminum tag is given us. I wear mine on my left wrist fastened by the mess-can chain. It is inscribed as follows;

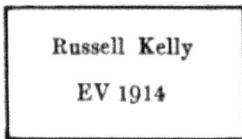

Front side

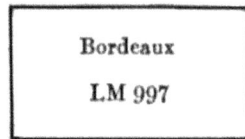

Reverse side

The other day the colonel inspected us and grouped us according to nationalities: there were eighteen groups. We were lined up and the colonel was giving instructions when an aeroplane appeared, so we promptly sought shelter. We all watch for an aeroplane and when one comes we generally are marched to quarters. Quite a number of 'planes are active but it is almost impossible to tell to which nation they belong. No chance is taken, however, and we quickly get under cover. It frequently happens that the sound of the motor is heard before the 'plane is located. Last Sunday night heavy cannonading was heard. It continued throughout the night, which was remarkably moonlight, and kept us awake the major part of the time. It must have been a big battle; I never heard its equal before.

When small detachments are shipped from here to join their

battalions in the trenches there is a great display of joyous feeling shown by the men. They yell, sing, dance and rough-house generally. One would imagine that they are going to a festival. The New York papers do not exaggerate when they say this Legion is a fighting crowd. There are just enough of each nationality so that one country fights another. There has been a couple of scraps here to date.

The chief cook for our section was an Italian and as he was dishing up poor stuff, we four got sore and told him he had better improve, but he did not take the hint. The kitchen is located very near the loft we sleep in, so one day when the meal was particularly poor we reached out of the door and heaved the whole business at him. It almost completely demolished the kitchen. A plate of meat and hot rice hit him on the head and he jumped into the path of a bowl of soup. He was a sorry looking *dago* when the avalanche ceased. We are getting good meals now. The other day we were nearly paralyzed when he had fried potatoes for us.

A detachment of about eighty Greeks left yesterday for the trenches. They were a very wild crowd and when they marched out of town they carried two Greek flags and were singing Greek songs. They had Greek officers. A number of the men had worked in the States. One was a waiter in the Hotel Knickerbocker, New York, but most of them had worked in railroad gangs.

I went to mass the other Sunday: it was served the same as in the States. The church is very old: the place for the altar is wider than the pew space. The main altar is set hack from the others and it only is railed off. In the space I mentioned as being wider than the pew section are two rows of pews, one on each side of the main aisle. They run at right angles to the altar and, I take it, are reserved for the elite of the town, as they are finely made and comfortable, not to mention their isolation. The regular pews are very uncomfortable, being straight-backed, while the board to kneel on is very narrow. The pews are placed close together which cramps one considerably. The organ is placed almost among the rafters.

The acoustic properties of the building are poor. The structure is of stone, the walls being very thick. Immense stone columns, placed at short intervals, support the roof. On the first column on the left hand side of the aisle, about twelve feet from the floor, a small pulpit is built and is reached by a circular staircase. The floor is of marble. Instead of tableaux, cheap pictures show the Stations of the Cross. Lamps and candles furnish the light: no provision is made for heat. The windows are of stained glass and rather artistic. There was only a scattering of people, mostly women in mourning. A few soldiers attended.

As I have said this is the Champagne country; vineyards exist in abundance and at the present time they need attention; the ground around each vine must be loosened. Most of the men are in the army, so nearly everyone in town turns out to work. Old men, old women, middle-aged women, young women, boys and girls and even children labour in the yards. I have seen grey-haired women bent almost double over the short three-foot hoe in use here. Everybody works, they work hard and with a will. From their appearance, the grapes will not suffer from lack of attention.

A few nights ago just as I was on the point of going to sleep a soldier came rushing through our quarters yelling "Fire." In two shakes of a lamb's tail we were all downstairs, formed in ranks and on double time in the direction of the fire, and as it was only a short distance off, we were soon there. As is the local custom, the house was set back and shut off from the road by an eighteen-inch brick and stone wall covered with cement. Next to, and in fact part of the house was the hay shed; some cavalry men were quartered here.

When we came into the courtyard the shed and nearest half of the top or second floor of the house were in flames. Already some of the furniture had been carried out from the ground floor rooms, and taking the hint, we rushed through the door-way to bring out more. It was one of the best houses in town and well furnished. By this time nearly everybody in town had arrived, but there was no sign of any fire fitting apparatus, and the fire was quickly destroying the house. Soon there were many triumphant cries, and with much gusto the Fire Department of Bouzy burst upon the scene, and was greeted by the crowd with many acclamations of joy.

The Fire Department was carried by eager hands, and seeing a couple of vacant inches, I took hold. Everybody was yelling and giving orders, so the department was carried all over the yard and frequently came near being deposited on the ground, when someone with an extra loud voice would tell of a more advantageous spot, so there the department would go. This procedure was kept up for about five minutes before the machine was placed.

It consisted of a heavy iron tank four feet long, three feet wide and two feet high with two cylinders and a long two-handled bar for the manpower. Soon the hose was arranged and men formed for a bucket-brigade. Think of it: a machine to which the water must be brought and then pumped through the hose to the blaze. It was a long time before the water arrived and we frequently had to suspend for lack of water. Smith mounted to the roof of the building and Larney was conspicuous on an adjoining roof. Just as Smith reached the roof a stream from a nearby house started to play, but lacked force enough to reach the flames; it landed directly on Smith and continued playing on him. In a short time he was drenched and the spray also wet Larney through.

Well, to make a long story short, the building was completely destroyed, but no damage was done to any nearby structure. Smith slept in his wet clothes and the next morning when he unrolled from his blanket a cloud of steam arose. He surely must have had an enjoyable evening trying to sleep.

The helmets worn by the firemen were of brass and resembled the German helmet, only lacking the spike. They were highly polished and quite showy.

CHAPTER 4

In the First Line Trenches

Somewhere in France (Bouzy),
March 7, 1915.
We were outfitted unexpectedly this evening and are busy
packing and getting rid of excess weight so as to start early
tomorrow morning for the trenches. The men are glad at the
prospect of getting into the game, and are making considerable
noise and having a high old time.

(Place Unknown),
Wednesday, March 10.
At half-past five o'clock last Monday morning we were up
and ready to start. We left Bouzy at a quarter to seven by the
town clock. After several rests we reached a fair-sized town and
had lunch: we were served hot coffee here. After a spell in the
trenches the men return to repose in this town.
We were divided here to be placed in different battalions, etc.,
and I was glad to learn that we were lucky enough to be sent
to a battalion which was then occupying the trenches. We left
town together and proceeded on our way which led through
the greatest vineyards I had yet seen. We paused in a barn for
a short time and started off again. There were about ten of us;
Smith and Larney were with me; Pavelka we left in Bouzy as he
is sick. I do not know what is the matter with him, but it does
not amount to much, whatever it is.
We finally arrived in what was once a town. I say once, because
as a town it ceases to exist. It had contained, I should say, about
two or three hundred houses. While in New York I had read
of the towns that were destroyed in the war, but the realization

exceeded my most elaborate ideas. There was not a building in the entire town which had not received its share of destruction. We walked through several streets looking for somebody to direct us but could find no one. The place seemed deserted; and what a scene of ruin. Here was the church with gaping holes in the roof and one side with four openings large enough to drive a team through. The other sides were battered and the steeple was blown off. It is impossible to convey any idea of the ruin which was everywhere seen. One row of four houses had the connecting walls completely destroyed. In the entire town there was not a house with its roof left, nor a pane of unbroken glass.

We finally located a sentinel who showed us headquarters, where we were assigned to our companies, etc. After lunch we were to proceed to our trench. While waiting for the repast an occasional shell whistled by and exploded a short distance beyond. Very pleasant, I assure you. We finished the meal and were ready. A short distance from the kitchen, to my great surprise, we entered the famous trenches. Here we were at last. I wish I could express my feelings when I realized where I was.

It was simply the connecting trench which allowed the men from the line trenches to proceed to the kitchen and get the meals. The Germans have a disagreeable habit of shelling these trenches at meal time and quite a few accidents have occurred in them. They are about five feet deep and very narrow. The earth is thrown up on both sides, so they are quite deep. They curve in a horrible fashion and it was not long before I was dizzy. Meanwhile an occasional shell went merrily by. The trenches are so narrow that it is difficult for two men to pass. We continued on and passed the entrance to the second line: after a while we stopped. Where do you suppose we were? We were at last actually in the first line of trenches.

We were taken to the lieutenant, who assigned us to our squads. The first thing we did was to place our rifles in holes in the trench facing the Germans. I looked over the top of the trench in the direction of the enemy but could not distinguish much, as it was beginning to get dark. They were there, however, there was no question as to that for an occasional bullet whistled by. An intermittent fire is kept up continually by both sides. Larney and I were put into the 15th squad and Smith in the 14th. We

41

were assigned to our quarters.

The firing line faces the Germans in a zigzag way. There is a trench running parallel to and back of it. They are connected by trenches in which are placed the living quarters of the men. There are two eaves or huts opposite each other in an alley. Of course they are underground. They are about three and a half to four feet high and about twelve feet deep. There are six men in ours. When lying down it is impossible to stretch one's legs out, consequently you are pretty well cramped after sleeping.

I was tired after our long march, so prepared to turn in, but found that we were to be on guard during the night. We turned out presently and I was placed with another fellow in a trench about twenty yards in advance of the main one. We were in back of steel shields with our rifles loaded and on the watch for a German. The fellow I was with was an Italian, so there was little conversation between us. We were there two hours and it was very cold. We saw nothing alarming. Both sides exchanged shots occasionally. I was very glad to be relieved, as a cold wind was blowing.

We went into the guard room and it was not long before I wished I was on post again. There was no fire in this cave and the ledge upon which we sat was about four inches wide. It was also cold in there. Finally we went out on patrol. We put the bayonets on our guns and laid down on the earth. I was in this position two and a half hours. Let me here state that I think I have enjoyed two and a half hours more at other times during my career. This sharp, cold wind continued, so after a while I was naturally chilled. There was no danger, however, as I estimated that the nearest bullet which passed us was at least twenty feel distant.

Nothing happened and at last we returned. I was very sleepy and in due time turned in. After sleeping about an hour and a half I was awakened as the captain wished to inspect the new men. After the inspection I had a good sleep: slept most of the day and all the night. It is rather uncomfortable in the cramped position but it is possible to keep warm when under the blanket.

The meals are good, but only lukewarm, as they have to be carried quite a distance. During the next day we left the trenches and returned to the town to repose. We are here now for eight

French houses ruined by Germans

days. It is very comfortable here. Another American was put in our squad; he is from Boston; has been in France five years and the Legion five months; in the trenches three months. He is a fine fellow.[1]

At present, things are very quiet. I think we made quite a record; from a reserve training station, put in the first line trenches and the first night there put on patrol and two days after that sent with the battalion on repose.

After this letter I will not be allowed to send any mail to any place for about a month.

Well, mother, I am nearly a full fledged soldier now. You would be surprised to know how glad I am to be where I am.

> Somewhere in France,
> March 15, 1915.

This is a good picture of the actual sights where I am now. Whole towns are like that shown on the other side. All well.

> Russell.

> Verzenay,
> April 9, 1915.

On March 26th we returned to the trenches, and the routine was the same as before, just the continual rifle and artillery fire and very close watching of the enemy. The trenches are dry now and fairly comfortable. We are all in tip-top shape and enjoying ourselves; the only thing we want is some action.

We are located in a place called Verzenay, which is about ten *kilometres* (six and a quarter miles) north of Bouzy. The first line trenches that we occupy are about five *kilometres* (three miles) north of the town. Verzenay is on the side of a high hill, the trenches being in the valley; a grand view of the town is had from the trenches.

I should judge the town has, normally, four to five thousand inhabitants. The Germans throw ten to fifteen shells into it daily, but they do little damage, and more than half of the civil population has remained here.

We were scheduled to leave town one night for the third line of defence and had our packs made up when in came a fellow who wanted to see the Americans. He was an American from the Second *Régiment étrangère*, and had been transferred at his

---

1. Kenneth Weeks of New Bedford, Mass. Killed June 16th.

own request, and as the authorities are following a plan of segregation by nations, he was sent to our squad. I was agreeably surprised to learn that he had been at Virginia Military Institute; he is Kniffin Y. Rockwell. His arrival brought our number up to five.

In due time we left and during the night reached our destination. They were the usual huts dug into the side of a slight terrace supporting the canal. They are about four feet high and six feet wide and long enough to accommodate a squad of fifteen men. They have been in use since the beginning of the war and fresh straw has been put into them at intervals. The old straw, however, has not been removed and when the men change quarters they leave behind them all discarded junk, so you can imagine the condition they are in. When I first arrived I tried to clean up, but the deeper I got into the straw the stronger the philosophy impressed itself on me that *"what one doesn't know won't hurt one,"* so I put back the straw and let it go at that.

There are a great number of rats and mice in the huts and the first night an energetic rat loosened a mass of earth above my head and it fell directly upon me. It gave me a great start as my first thoughts pictured a company of Germans on us. These rodents are a great nuisance on account of their large numbers and I have often wished there was a Pied Piper amongst us.

There is one man in the company who does not share my feelings. He is an Italian who is used to a strange diet. Every morning about nine o'clock he sits down and spreads out his victims of the night: they generally number five or six. He skins these and as he is a friend of the cook they are roasted for him. There is no question of his liking for them because we always have more than enough to eat. I have seen many strange things over here, but the cold-bloodedness of this fairly turns one's stomach.

There is not any regular schedule pursued here, but they always manage to keep us busy. During the second day Pavelka joined us from the hospital, which made the number six. This fellow is very handy and volunteered to make us a base ball. For the centre of the ball he used the business end of a cartridge and on this wound worsted and thread alternately. For a cover he cut up a leather *puttee* and sewed it on the ball. The complete article was really very good and it rivalled Spalding's Official

League Ball. Old A. G. would have given considerable for it for exhibition purposes, but he will never get it Home-run Scanlan, the heavy hitter, drove it into the canal and we lost it. He also broke up the game, much to the chagrin of the entire company who had gathered around to see us play. We had fun while it lasted, and we intend to make another one when we go back to the canal.

Aeroplanes are very numerous. There are so many that it became necessary to resume the aeroplane guard. Each section takes turns at this and it lasts from sunrise to sunset. Every time a German aircraft flies within range we fire at it. This occurs many times and considerable ammunition is used but no damage done. These machines warn us of their approach before they are located as the sound of the motor carries a great distance. Both armies shoot at the 'planes with cannon also.

It is quite interesting to follow the course of an aeroplane. Take a German one, for instance. We may be cleaning up when the faint whir of a motor is heard. Work ceases and all eyes try to locate the machine. It proves to be an approaching German 'plane. When the probable range is computed our artillery opens fire. The report of the piece is heard and we look in the vicinity of the aeroplane for the result. In a couple of seconds a puff of smoke is seen and shortly after the noise of the bursting shell reaches us. It is almost impossible to hit it. I have seen a great number fired at, but as yet, with no results.

Another thing to be remarked upon is the intrepidity of the aviators. They don't seem to pay any attention to the bombardment (if we may call it such). One beautiful afternoon while I was in the first line, a French aeroplane made for the enemies' lines. The Germans saw it coming and opened fire, using three pieces. The sky was cloudless, so I counted the puffs of smoke: they appeared all around the 'plane, but in spite of this the airman continued on his mission and actually got out of range behind the guns. All told there were sixty-eight shells thrown. For fifteen minutes after, it was possible to count the puffs. I have often wondered when the shells explode near an aeroplane and do not damage it, how it is that the concussion does not in some way injure the delicate parts of the machine. We have not seen an aerial combat, but all root for one.

On our first repose here in town we were treated to a bath: it was a great event. A soldier holds a hose with a sprinkler arrangement on the end and two others man the pump. First we are allowed a little water to get up a lather, then the master of ceremonies at the hose bellows a command and the boys at the pump bend to their work with a will, with the result that there is a free-for-all fight to get into the spray. It is rather a crude method, but as the water is hot we are very thankful for it. I had my second yesterday and we hope to bathe daily at the canal.

This canal reminds me greatly of the old Erie, save for the locks. Changing levels is accomplished by one single lock as against the single and double locks used on the Erie. Canal boat fleets are unknown in this country: the boats travel singly and are towed by horses. Considering the depth and width of the canal and the general appearance of the banks, one can almost imagine he is travelling through New York state on the old waterway. The type of boat used is practically the same as ours, save that over here they are somewhat larger and with a more pointed bow.

The other night Weeks took us out to dinner: the meal was served in the home of one of the native vineyard workers. We all filed into the kitchen of the house. This room was located on the ground floor and had a window opening onto the street. It served also as the pantry, dining room, and was also used for minor purposes. It was about ten by twelve feet. A common kitchen table occupied the centre of the room under a hanging oil lamp. There were eight chairs (the majority rickety) scattered around, and the deep window sill would accommodate three persons. Into the corner opposite the main door was fitted a triangular closet which accommodated odds and ends; the wine supply was kept here. Curtains decorated the window; the floor was bare. They used a good range.

Weeks was acquainted with the family as he had dined here throughout the winter when on repose. They also did his and other soldiers' washing and the clothes were hung in this room on lines from the walls to dry; consequently one was uncomfortable until seated. After a while our host gave his order and the woman went to purchase the food. Meanwhile children of the family were constantly coming and going. After the sixth had made his appearance I grew confused and decided not to try to keep track of them. They certainly were numerous, and

KNIFFIN Y. ROCKWELL.

starting from four feet six they descended in regular intervals of six inches down to the young baby, making a natural stairway for Father Time.

The food came at last; it was a chicken and some incidentals. The next thing was to prepare the chicken for the pot. The good housewife searched high and low for a knife, and failing to locate one borrowed Smith's famous weapon (he paid six *sous* for it in Lyon at a bazaar). Ah! I forgot. She singed the fowl first over the table around which we were seated. This was accomplished by means of burning newspapers, the ashes of which fell into the wine. We did not mind this, only the smell of burning hair was rather disagreeable. I had recovered from this, when, picture my chagrin, the good lady started to butcher the bird right under our noses and placidly strewed the table with the chicken's guts. I think grape picking trains the hands to quick, vigorous action; anyhow, the way those giblets and other parts of the chicken's anatomy were flying around caused us to dodge continually, and with great foresight I placed my hand over the glass to protect the wine.

The lady was not an expert butcher; when she could not locate a joint the members were torn apart by main strength. As for the flesh, it was actually ripped off in shreds and the whole business thrown into a pot. Smith's heart was almost broken as the blade of his knife was bent all out of shape: it was ruined. The meal consisted of rice, soup, fried chicken and bread, with coffee at the end. It was very tasty, indeed. What struck me forcibly was the way the children ate. They came in just long enough to swallow a few mouthfuls. Through carelessness I think the young folks are not receiving the proper amount of nourishment. Anyway the children of France do not shape up as being sturdy. We all enjoyed the novel incident greatly.

We eventually got to the first line again and occupied the same hut as on our previous stay. There were seven of us in there, six Americans and the corporal. It was not wide enough to lie cross ways, so we slept at an angle. It reminded me of the story of the six men in one bed; when a man became tired lying on one side and gave the signal to turn, all turned at once and if any one failed to hear the signal it broke up the party. This was the case here; we were cramped to an uncomfortable degree. The first night we were disturbed by a great racket. It proved to be Smith forcing Larney back into his proper location. It might be well to remark here that Larney is a considerable sleeper. He talks almost nightly and would you believe me, back in Bouzy he actually sang one verse of "My Country, 'Tis of Thee." It was in a far away, hollow voice, but he carried the tune fairly well. Some nights we grow alarmed over his welfare; he groans and mumbles so.

At the first line we are on guard every other night, and as the weather was cold it was not very enjoyable. One night I was on guard from one a. m. to three a. m. with Larney. We were in a trench running at right angles from the main one and about twenty feet from it. It is so arranged that the earth is on a level with our eyes. You would be surprised to know how hard it is to keep awake. Even as near the enemy as we are, an almost unconquerable desire to sleep overcomes us. It must be that the constant searching and the straining of the eyes into the darkness hypnotizes one, but be this as it may, it required a great effort to keep awake. We all complain of this.

On the night I speak about, I was struggling to keep awake when all of a sudden my heart almost stopped beating. I was thoroughly wide awake instantly: I could have sworn that there were two figures directly in front of me about one hundred and fifty feet away. One seemed to be standing and the other kneeling, and as we maintain a trench running parallel to the main one and about one hundred and fifty feet beyond, my mind pictured all kinds of things. I watched them intently and they seemed to be working at something, but in the uncertain light it was maddening.

The large figure appeared to be motionless but the small one seemed to rise and bend like a man at a pump. This continued for what seemed ages. I am well aware that at night objects take strange forms, but I could not account for these. Our rifles are constantly loaded and cocked while on guard and I was tempted to take a shot at it, but I wanted to see them actually move before I fired. I looked over and saw Larney observing the same thing.

We talked it over and decided that it was part of the landscape; the next morning we went into the trench and came to the conclusion that it was two trees.

Another time while on guard in the second line position, I was looking out of a small port hole in the trench. I had just come to the conclusion that guard duty was a waste of time when I saw what looked to be a figure crawling slowly under the barbed wires in front of the trench.

It was a wretched night, raining and very dark. I could have sworn that this was really a man. I almost pictured him freeing himself from the barbs. I thought a better view would be gained from over the trench, so I noiselessly climbed up until my head was clear of the earth, but it was impossible to see when my eyes were above the surface of the earth, so I got back again.

The object was still in the same position. Would you believe I actually kept my eyes glued on the thing for nearly two hours. A number of lights were sent up by both sides, but their positions were such they did not help me. Finally, a German white light went up in a direct line with my eyes and the object. What do you think my creeping German was? Nothing but a frame to roll wire on. I certainly was disgusted when I made this discovery.

One cannot help imagining things. Everything keys the imagination up; the steady rifle fire, the occasional cannon, the bursting mines,, the flare of the night lights and distant bombardments all tend to put one in a condition to see anything.

It is interesting to observe the difference of speed between sight and sound. For instance, a cannon tar in our rear will discharge a shell; the flash is visible from the piece, the whir of the shell as it passes is heard, and the flash as it bursts is seen, then both reports sound almost simultaneous, the discharge of the gun and bursting of the shell. This, of course, only happens when one's position is almost in the middle of the trajectory.

Another idea of mine which was shattered by actual experience was the action of a bursting shell. From war pictures I drew the inference that at the moment a shell bursts it was possible to see the fragments; not so. The report of the piece is heard, then the whistle of the shell, a puff of smoke is seen and finally a loud report. That's all, but believe me there is a great deal of power in a shell.

In the second line the quarters were fair. Wide enough for us to stretch out and about five feet high. Each one accommodates a section. The condition of the straw was the same as described before. One night it began to rain and in about half an hour the rain soaked through the earth and dripped on us. We hung our shelter-halves up under the roof to catch the water. These covers performed their duty O. K., but the water leaked in all around them. The first night was not so bad, although the place was wet in spots. It rained during the second day and things became worse: the trenches were in an awful condition, the water being ankle deep in places and the mud beating Cedarhurst's best to a fare-you-well.

That night, however, was the worst of all. The rain was dripping through pretty steadily and it had begun to get the best of the tent covers in spite of the fact that we emptied them regularly. We eventually turned in and as an almost steady stream was dropping on my head I put my overcoat over it and grappled with Morpheus. I had him flat on his back and was about to rise to the cries of the spectators when my subconscious mind differentiated between the voice of applause and the wail of dismay. Instantly I was awake and poked my head out to see what the fuss was about, but the steady stream forced my cranium under the coat again.

Out of the confusion I gleamed that a tent cover had fallen with the weight of the water and drenched a Greek, two fellows down from me. He was very active vocally: I'll bet he cursed a few. We were all very uncomfortable. I was telling myself how good it was to be dry when I realized that I was not as dry as I might be. From my shoulders to my feet I was awash in three inches of water. It surely did feel fierce, but it was impossible to better the condition as everything was wet. It was only two a. m. and I prayed for daylight. We managed to dry out pretty well during the day.

I wish we had some of those new patented trench digging machines the World's Advance tells about, because I have dug about one thousand miles of trenches, or nearly that many. We are constantly digging new and repairing old trenches, so now we have an elaborate system of underground streets.

I certainly do feel fine and enjoy the life, but there is no question about it, war is an asinine thing.

CHAPTER 5

Removed to the Arras Secteur

(Place Unknown),
May 6. 1915.

For many days we knew something was in the wind, but what or when it would happen was a puzzle to all. Some said we were going back to Lyon for a repose, while others maintained we were bound for the Dardanelles. Finally we got orders to pack all our stuff and be ready to move during the night. About midnight, April 24th, a French regiment relieved us and we marched out of Verzenay. It was a very disagreeable night, and coupled with a chilly, penetrating fog and the rather forced march, we were more or less fatigued when we reached a small town at about five o'clock the next morning: our *escouade* (squad), the 15th, was assigned to a sort of cow shed. The ground was as hard as a rock and as cold. We turned in, but tired as we were, it was impossible to get much sleep, although we tried to sleep during the day. At five in the afternoon we went up town to see what the place was like; it was a small place with about six stores and overcrowded with soldiers.

When we got back I started to read periodicals received from New York. Outside there was a small yard with a squad kitchen on one side and our quarters on the other. I'll stop here a second to say a word about the men in our squad.

The corporal could be most anything but I think he is Arab-French; he is a quiet fellow and O. K. There are four *Légionnaires* with us; one of them has served fifteen years with the Legion and another about ten. These two are naturalized Frenchmen and fast friends. The old-timer has a huge beard and is a very quaint character. I enjoy watching him; he reminds me so much of those gnomes who used to interest me when I was small. The other fellow is short and very brown. The way they confide in each other is really ludicrous. When one has an imaginary illness he takes the other aside and they get their heads together and sympathize with each other; it is laughable. As they share their sorrows they also share their joys. You buy their kind of joy by the canteen full, and believe me they are a joyous pair. The old fellow has been joyous for about fifteen years.

The other two *Légionnaires* are Belgians and unimportant. Then we have two Italians who remind me of brigands. One is a big husky fellow and the other is a typical dramatic villain; good looking, dashing and all that stuff. We have an Italian kid with us, but he is only a nuisance. The two brigands take an interest in him to the extent of continually kicking and cuffing him around. Well, as I was reading the magazine I heard a noise in the yard and upon going out found the six-foot corporal slugging the five-foot five *Légionnaire*. I was glad to see it because the little fellow needs a beating. He talks too much. Weeks was out there and did not like the unevenness of the fight so he interfered. The big brigand then came up and hit the little *Légionnaire* a "beaut," knocking him across the yard. The little fellow got up just in time to be knocked back across the yard, and the big fellow was going to repeat the performance when Weeks interfered again.

By this time we were all out in the yard enjoying the fun. The argument got pretty hot and finally, as usual, the peacemaker got a wallop in the jaw. The American section acted as if they were all hit, and in fact they were when one of them was hit. In a fraction of a second it was the biggest free-for-all I was ever in or hope to be in. We battled around the yard to a fare-you-well and in no time the guard was on the scene with fixed bayonets, but we still kept on.

In a lull in the action I happened to look around in time to see the villainous looking bandit picking up a brick. I made a bee-line for him and in no time had received a good clout on my bean for my trouble. The guards eventually separated us, but the Americans carried the day. They started to take me to the lock-up but I landed at the infirmary and had my head bandaged. They locked Pavelka up, but he should have come with me, as a friend of the bandits hit him on the forehead with a dish pan.

He needed bandaging and soon was sent back for treatment. We all shook hands and called it square.

The next day we marched to the railroad and came north. It was a wretched trip as we were packed closely in freight cars and it took twenty-four hours to come two hundred *kilometres*, being about one hundred and twenty-five miles. We left the cars at a town called Aubigny, which is about six miles due west of the village of La Targette, but we located in a town nearer the front. At night we marched to the trenches and worked there. It was very dangerous: the outposts being about fifty yards apart. One night the second fellow from me was hit in the stomach. It is good to work under such conditions, as work takes the mind from the bullets; inaction under fire is a terrible strain on the nerves.

We were in the trenches three days, worked all day and at night we went out on the field and laid down four hours at a stretch, to guard against a surprise. To make matters worse it rained and the mud was a foot deep in places. We went back to a small town, arriving there at ten a. m.

We have everything in abundance. I have seen fellows throw shirts and other articles away, rather than wash them, as new ones are always given. There is actually more than enough of everything. We are living like princes.

I was glad to hear that my letter from Bouzy was received. Allowance must be made for the writing as it was done on a two-by-four-foot plank, which I straddled, my feet dangling. We Americans were all interested in the statement in the letter to me, that it has been said the Germans would treat Foreign *Légionnaires* who were not citizens of France as irregular soldiers; and the suggestions made for us to observe in case of capture will be followed.

CHAPTER 6

Battle of Artois; at La Targette and Neuville St. Vaast

Somewhere near Aubigny,
May 16. 1915.

On Sunday morning. May 9th, we were— routed out at one o'clock and marched to the trenches, reaching the third line at sunrise, and at five o'clock our artillery increased its already very severe bombardment,—the continual rumble and vibration being beyond description. This lasted until ten o'clock and as soon as it stopped, Battalion C in our section left the trenches, charging with the bayonet.

They carried the trenches with great loss. I understand the Germans were panic stricken by the bombardment and one of their battalions was buried as the trenches collapsed under our heavy artillery fire.

Battalion A followed C and lost a great many; there are two Americans in A, one of them is O. K. while the other was shot twice, in the shoulder and in the leg.

Our Battalion B left the trenches right after A under a heavy rifle and machine gun fire, the ground we crossed being well strewn with dead and dying of Battalions C and A. We charged across fields in a line of skirmishes, and I will never be able to satisfy myself how so many of us got through safely.

When we reached the first line of German trenches we found them battered and destroyed by our bombardment. Soon after crossing them our first stop was in the shelter of a road. Here the good looking bandit, the fellow who hit me with the brick, got reckless and tried to survey the landscape; he was killed instantly by a bullet through the heart. No convulsive tossing of the arms one reads about or sees in the movies—he just sank down and it was all over. Soon after we left this position, the other bandit was shot through the leg. There was absolutely no ill feeling between us on account of our scrap.

We then laid down on the ground and soon the Germans got our range; six men close to me were hit; so we started on again.

The German artillery had opened on us, and the suspense of lying there and waiting to be hit is indescribable. The shells were bursting all around me and one rushed by so close that I actually think a chunk of solidified air hit me on the forehead; anyway, something bruised my forehead. I rushed over and got into the hole, it was five feet deep. I happened to be looking where four men were lying, when a shell blew the four of them to dust.

In my letter from Lyon I mentioned three brothers from Argentina; they were inseparable even in death; they were killed side by side.

We finally took the crest of a hill, it was dusk and we dug ourselves in.

I shall never forget the picture displayed as I looked back across the field in the fading light. It is a nightmare: during the entire night the cries of the wounded rang out. I had a pleasant bedfellow,—a corporal and he lay in the trench, only two feet away. He actually fascinated me. I could not help looking at his brains which stuck out of the back of his neck, exactly like two horns. During the next day they gradually melted until at nightfall they had slid entirely off his neck. Grand, grand indeed, is this butchery they call war!

During the night we were on the watch, and at times the fire from the enemy, aided by the German night-lights, was severe.

As day broke Monday we were ready for the counter attack, which was sure to come and it came early and fierce. Their artillery shelled us in a most desperate manner, and men were killed and wounded in large numbers and very close to me; and again the suspense of expecting to be hit by a shell was horrible.

Bavarian troops were opposite and they made a rush for us, and I am bound to acknowledge that no human beings could have shown more bravery and determination than they did: but our artillery was most effective, and we stood firm in our trenches and smeared them. Their counter attacks all failed and that night we still held the trenches we had dug.

We were entirely out of water both Sunday and Monday, and as a consequence suffered very much.

Early the next morning, before daybreak, reserves took our places and what was left of our regiment returned to the rear for reorganisation.

I laugh when I try to think of civilization. But with all we must admit it is a great world and I do not regret that I am here.

Somewhere near Aubigny,
May 20, 1915.

A sergeant was commanding our company, all the officers having been killed or wounded. Our captain was a very game man; he led us without a sword or any side arms, only using his swagger stick. He was killed by a shell.

We advanced by sections. When the order came we jumped up, and carrying a sack as a shield, ran about one hundred feet,— and talk about Ty Cobb sliding into second base, it isn't a circumstance to the way I hit the ground. And what a strain it was on the nerves waiting for our turn to advance again, fellows all around being hit. In a couple of cases I have seen men almost lifted from the ground, so hard were they struck. One fellow very near me was hit and began to squeal, almost immediately a second bullet hit him and he made for the rear on all fours crying like a child. The field was full of such sights.

But compared to the shells the bullets axe nothing: give me most anything but an artillery bombardment. I cannot figure out how the five of us missed being hit.

The prisoners we took were well fed and clothed, but are sick of the war.

After the attack we were quartered in Mont St. Eloi, about two miles west of La Targette, but as it was in range and the Germans shelled us, we were sent ten miles to the rear to await recruits.

Our regiment lost heavily in killed and wounded, not half coming back. The little Italian kid I previously mentioned was too frightened to leave our trenches.

The six Americans of our squad, Larney, Rockwell, Pavelka, Smith, Weeks and myself passed through safely, except Rockwell who was shot in the leg. We learned he was cared for by our field ambulance.

CHAPTER 7

To the Rear for Recruiting

(Place Unknown),
June 10, 1915.

Soon after we were located at the rear to await recruits the general commanding our division reviewed us and distributed five military medals.

We have a new captain in the place of the one who was killed; he is a Swede and is very military; he has us drilling a great deal, and works us pretty hard, considering that we have smelt powder in the true sense of the term.

We have just learned that Italy has entered the war; also, that an American merchantman has been torpedoed. We would like to see the United States keep out of the war if it can.

On May 20th we returned to a location near the front, and lately many German prisoners have passed us. One day as many as eight hundred went by; they looked well. By a strange coincidence the same Bavarian troops who faced us in Champagne are against us here, and yesterday we recognized a man in their ranks who deserted from us in Champagne. I guess it is all over with him; it should be.

It seems that our effort of May 9th was more successful than that of the British. The German prisoners say they cannot stand our artillery fire. I don't blame them, as the French 75 centimetre field piece has proved to be the wonder of the war.

We are all well; in fact I never felt better in my life.

I have just received the packages from New York and am thankful for them. Socks are very desirable as we are on our feet a great part of the time and I can rest easy now that I am well stocked with them. The soup cubes were fine: we make soup every night before turning in. One of the toothbrushes was broken in transit but the other comes in handy as the one I brought from home is about used up. I am keeping the combs, but do not use them, as during the hot weather our hair is cut very close with the machine. Some fellows have their heads shaved, but I think that is going too far. This idea of having the hair cut short is a good one as it is very warm here now.

We spent four days in the trenches to the left of the ones the Legion occupied prior to the attack of May 9th, Skipper Pavelka and I went all through the devastated German trenches. I could find scarcely anything as we were there nearly three weeks after the attack and countless French soldiers had searched before us. I found some envelopes and wrappers for parcel post packages with the German postage stamps attached, and I send these to you; it will be seen the letters bear Bavarian postage stamps, and are directed to Bavarian infantry soldiers.

The German trenches were built much better than ours. Some of the huts in which the men lived were twenty feet underground. They used a great number of dirt sacks: there must be a shortage of strong material in Germany, as these sacks were made mostly from cheap, light calico which was hardly strong enough to hold the earth.

They had an extensive system of mines and we made the attack just in time as Pavelka and I investigated the saps with the aid of a candle. They were all loaded and wired ready to be set off. One of them had been exploded. The Germans lost their bearings in digging, because the hole was actually nearer their own lines than it was to ours. They used a tremendous charge and the explosion must have been terrific for the result reminded me of the crater of a volcano; it was easily thirty feet deep.

Our bombardment before the attack of May 9th had played havoc with the German trenches; a great number of the roofs on the huts had fallen during the cannonading burying alive all the occupants. Around these places the stench was horrible. All through these trenches was evidence of heavy losses on the part of the Germans; at intervals, arms and legs projected from the walls and floor of the trenches, and all in all it was a pretty gruesome journey.

As a result of May 9th our line is advanced over two miles, but the Germans hold a dangerous position on the side of a large hill and it will be hard work chasing them off.

We have been out to dig trenches a couple of times and believe me we sure do work. Imagine getting up and working on the ground about two hundred and fifty yards from the German line with them shooting all the time. Work! you bet the men work with a will and it does not take long to get a good trench dug. They have a poor system here. We walk about seven miles from this town where we are now to the first line, dig a trench and walk back. We leave at six p. m. and get back at five a. m.— the idea of walking seven miles to work.

There is not much left of the Legion of May 9th; the Italians have been liberated to return to their own army. Our company had fifty-five men out of a full company of two hundred and fifty, but we expect to be filled up again with the men from Valbonne and Lyon. I should judge one thousand have already been sent up here from those places.

Well, this war is a great game. The next person who mentions the glories of war should be jumped on with both feet. Picture the charge with the band playing and the men singing—what tommy-rot. In the first place the instruments never get near the actual fighting, and in the second place the men at that time don't care a bang for a song.

We have some fun with the boxing gloves, a new set having been sent to us from Paris. It is surprising to know how many good boxers there are around here. The other day two *Zouaves* who weighed about one hundred and eighty pounds each turned up and were very clever. One had boxed for the amateur championship of Tunis. They would give many professional fighters a run for the money. Two French cavalrymen had a bout that resulted in a knockout.

Time surely does fly: here it is nearly eight months since the old Goddess of Liberty disappeared into the distance in New York bay. It does not seem possible.

The ball that hit Rockwell's leg just missed the bone, so he is recovering rapidly and hopes to be back with us soon.

We are all in the best of health and getting plenty to eat. We are unanimous in wishing for the war to end soon. Those who clamour for war the most in the States are those who know nothing about it. War is an asinine waste and I take my hat off to President Wilson for his level headedness.[1]

(Place Unknown)
June 15, 1915.

Dear Dad:

All well. Received your letter of May 30, 1915. We were there all right. Will write later. Love to all.

Russell.

The First Regiment was cited in the official Order of the Day, as follows:

The First Foreign Regiment of the Second *régiment de Marche*, ordered May 9th under the command of Lieutenant Colonel Cot to make a bayonet charge on a strong German position, went into the attack, the officers leading in front of the men, with a superb gallantry, gaining, with only brief stops, several kilometres of ground, in spite of an extremely strong resistance of the enemy and a violent fire from his machine guns.

Le Figaro of Paris, May 13th, 1915, contains an article from which the following translation is an extract, under the heading, "*Nos succés du 9 mai dans le secteur, Carency—Neuville.*"

The attack on La Targette, led by a division of the army corps from the neighbourhood, mentioned in the army order, was conducted with a remarkable boldness and was a complete success.

The artillery had, by its fire, demolished a large part of the barbwire and other accessories of the defence. A certain number of *mitrailleuses* had escaped destruction, and the enemy continued to hold them.

At the first assault our infantry reached the border of the woods, but it was stopped there by fire on the flank. The infantry resumed the attack immediately and took a part of the trenches at ten o'clock; which it held, and at a quarter past eleven took all of La Targette and three hundred and fifty prisoners, many pieces of seventy-seven and a large number of *mitrailleuses*.

Holding La Targette, they were masters of the cross-roads of Arras-Béthune and Mont Saint-Eloi-Neuville.

---

1. The above was the last letter received; the communication on the following page was written on a military postal card.

They reformed rapidly, thanks to the heroic work of the engineer corps, and advanced upon Neuville.

This village presents itself in the form of a point. It was, as an officer expressed it, 'a real bundle of *mitrailleuses* and of lance-bombs.' The assault was, however, made and about three o'clock we attacked the church.

From each loopholed house, from each cellar organized into a covered trench, the enemy fired on our men. They conquered, however, house by house, half of the village, and in spite of all counter-attacks we held the captured ground. It was a tremendous struggle amidst the wreckage and smoke.

Every minute augmented the number of prisoners. We saw them rush out from their hiding places, reckless of safety, stupefied by our bombardment, dumbfounded by our dash, and in a moment, towards the other side of the village some columns were detached, and our cavalry conducted the prisoners towards the rear, to the great joy of the population.

Behold the road of Béthune: a new attack. The battalions in the lead scaled the slope at the east and behind them, the others arriving, killed and despatched all whom they encountered.

Our officers fell in great numbers. Of four chiefs of battalions there was not more than one left. One of the colonels is seriously wounded. The general of the brigade who led in advance of his troops, had his chest pierced by a ball.

It made no difference, they went on with redoubled ardour. The men came at a gymnastic pace, leaped over the trenches, attacked the crest and the very crown of the crest.

The courier started, reached the telephonic post and sent in an account. One can hardly believe it. It was done; more than four *kilometres* gained (two and a half miles).

Never before in this war of a siege which has lasted for seven months, has a like success been obtained either by the Germans or by US. A German colonel was taken prisoner at his post of command. Behind our victorious battalions, our forces gathered up and unearthed from their burrows hundreds of Germans. We destroyed or captured, substantially, a whole brigade.

CHAPTER 8

Supplementary

BATTLE OF ARTOIS—SOUCHEZ—HILL NO. 119.

No communication has been received from Russell Kelly since his postal card of June 15th, mentioned in the foregoing chapter. He took part with his regiment in the battle on the following day, and since then has been missing, and his name is still carried on the French War Office Official list of missing. As the reader may be interested in the subsequent occurrences, the following facts are given.

The Battle of Waterloo occurred on June 18, 1815, and as its centenary approached the public expected an unusual effort would be made in commemoration of that momentous event.

Whether or not the warring powers gave any heed to this circumstance, is not known, but preparations were made by the Allies before that date, on a most extensive scale, for a formidable effort to break through the German lines in France.

On June 15th the soldiers of the Legion were each given one hundred extra rounds of ammunition; these they carried in their *meusettes* or haversacks; their belts contained the regular allowance of two hundred and fifty rounds. New underclothing and shirts were furnished to the troops that day, so that those who might be wounded would be less liable to contract the dreaded tetanus. A special mass was celebrated that day and the Catholic soldiers attended to their religious duties.

Many of the soldiers made provision for the event of disaster. John Smith left an envelope with instructions that it be opened if he did not return from the attack. When it was opened it was found to contain a statement that his real name was John Earl Fike, and it gave his mother's name and address, with a request that she be notified of his fate. Lawrence Scanlan also left written directions for notifying his mother and Russell Kelly sent the postal card given in chapter 7.

The extreme northerly end of the French line of battle was then at Souchez and that position was held by one battalion of *Zouaves*, about one thousand men; next to them was the Second *régiment de Marche* of the First Foreign Regiment, consisting of about four thousand men. In this last regiment was of course our five Americans, the sixth, Rockwell, being then in hospital.

An Irish regiment was on the extreme southerly end of the English line, and thus joined with the French *Zouaves*.

Pieces of white muslin were pinned to the backs of many of the *Légionnaires* (they advanced without knapsacks) so they could be distinguished from the enemy. This precaution was taken for the reason that in the a tack on May 9th, a serious delay occurred because the observers attached to the French 75 guns were unable to distinguish the French from the Germans.

A despatch bearer who had messages from the officers at the front stating that the Legion bad made a great advance, and directing that the range of the guns be changed so as to pass over the French troops, was killed and the messages undelivered. When the soldiers of the Legion reached this line of range of their own guns, many ran into the fire, and the others were compelled to hold back until another messenger was despatched.

After a terrific bombardment of the German trenches for several days, the French troops left their trenches at eight o'clock in the morning of June 16th, for the attack.

Ladders were in the front line trenches to enable the soldiers to get out quickly; a ladder being provided for every five men.

It will be remembered that on May 9th Battalion C led the advance, followed by A, and then B, but on June 16th it was Battalion B, containing these five Americans, that was first to leave in its sector. It faced a very severe fire from machine guns, rifles and shrapnel. The men ran forward in a line, at a distance of about a yard apart, and many fell before the first line of German trenches were reached. These had been destroyed by the French artillery and vacated by the enemy, and little of the barbed wire defences remained. However, the broken ground where those trenches had been afforded some slight shelter and advantage was taken of it to rest and rearrange the line.

They then rushed for the second line of trenches, which were strongly defended, having many machine guns in action; the French lost heavily before reaching these trenches, those who did safely reach them had a hand to hand fight with the Germans. It was here that Paul Pavelka received a bayonet wound in his leg and Lawrence Scanlan was severely wounded in his leg and foot by rifle fire, Russell Kelly received what a companion described as "a clean wound in his left shoulder that did not seem to be serious." All trace of John Smith and Kenneth Weeks was lost at this point. Weeks carried the supply of hand grenades for his section.

But in spite of all resistance the French captured those trenches, and pushed on to the next, where they had another desperate hand to hand encounter but which they also captured.

This division of the French army then drove its way through Cabaret Rouge, which has been frequently mentioned in the despatches. It is only a wine shop on the road to Arras and on the southern outskirts of Souchez.

In spite of the German artillery and machine gun fire they continued to advance, driving the enemy before them, capturing many, and taking Hill No. 119 to the southeast of Souchez. Pavelka and Scanlan, who lay wounded at the second line of trenches, could plainly see their comrades, distinguished by the pieces of white muslin on their backs, fighting their way, step by step, up Hill 119.

The division pushed on towards Givenchy, which is about a mile east of Souchez; but the Germans were able to attack them on their left flank, and the German artillery established a curtain of fire and thus cut off re-enforcements. The rest of the line did not advance as fast nor as far as the portion that included this battalion, so before the day was over the Germans had surrounded the men who were so advanced, and subjected them to a most severe artillery and machine gun fire.

The men so surrounded numbered about five hundred and they held out until the afternoon of the next day, when, with every man remaining wounded and exhausted from thirst, they were all captured with the exception of some few who were able to conceal themselves within the German lines, it having been since reported that some of the men avoided capture in that way.

Every officer in the regiment was killed.

The battle that day resulted in a net gain to the Allies of about two miles in depth over a front of about two miles; which gain was held for about six months, when the Germans recovered nearly one mile.

FRENCH

Paris,
Thursday, June 17, 10 p. m.

Great activity along the entire front during the last two days is reported in today's despatches. The fighting to the north of Arras has assumed an extremely violent character since yesterday. Infantry actions have been numerous and vigorous, while the artillery duel has been exceptionally violent and uninterrupted. We have achieved important gains which were almost all maintained despite furious counter attacks, which were repeated today with renewed vigour.

Yesterday and today we advanced steadily toward Souchez from the northwest, the south-west and the west. Further to the south we have gained a footing in the park of the Carleul Château, where the enemy had been making use of the moat around the *château* as a defensive base. We captured the Souchez cemetery and gained some ground on the slopes to the southeast of Souchez (Hill No. 119) following several brilliant charges. The results achieved yesterday were extended today.

After our infantry had delivered some extremely vigorous attacks, which were most efficaciously supported by the firing of almost three hundred thousand shells by our artillery, it was compelled to face, during the night of Wednesday, several violent counter attacks made by important hostile forces. These attacks were repulsed along the entire front, the only point evacuated by us being a small wood which we captured yesterday morning south of Hill No. 119 and which the enemy's artillery made it impossible for us to hold.

In these engagements the Germans used eleven divisions, which all suffered extremely heavy losses. On our side the losses were also serious.

The morale of our troops continues to be perfect. The number of prisoners captured by us exceeds six hundred, including more than twenty officers.

GERMAN

Berlin,
Thursday, June 17.

The British and French continued yesterday their attempts to break through our lines. North of La Bassée Canal the British, overpowered by Westphalians and Saxons, after a hand-to-hand fight, were forced to beat a speedy retreat into their positions. South of Souchez the French succeeded in penetrating into our positions over a width of about 600 metres, and obtained a foothold. Fighting still continues. At all other points they were repulsed with sanguinary losses.

French

Paris,
Saturday, June 19, 10 p. m.
In the sector to the north of Arras we have continued our action and on several points gathered the fruits of the favourable engagements of the last few days. . . .
We hold the slopes of Hill 119 where our troops are maintaining themselves, clinging to the ground beyond the last German trenches, notwithstanding counter attacks by the enemy. To the south of these slopes our front has been carried forward to the northeast of the Labyrinth.

German

Berlin,
Saturday, 3 p. m.
Several French attacks on the Lorette Hills, on both sides of Neuville and northeast of Arras broke down. We cleared a few trench sections which we had previously lost, of all enemies.

Account of battle from the *New York American*, August 7, 1915.

Three Americans in Legion Captured
Orderly Describes Brilliant Charge Against Germans by Squad from U. S. in French Ranks

By International News Service
Paris, August 6.
It now seems certain the three Americans of the famous First Regiment of the Foreign Legion who have been missing since the big fight north of Arras on June 16th are prisoners in Germany. They are Kenneth Weeks, Russell Kelly, and John Smith. The news was brought to Paris by an orderly of the regiment's

colonel, who, while lying in the field of battle with a shattered leg, was picked up by the German Red Cross. His leg was amputated in a field hospital and he was recently repatriated.

According to the orderly, Battalion B, of the Legion in which these Americans were lighting on June 16th, broke far through the German lines left of Cabaret Rouge. The Germans reformed on both sides, attacking in force, and by the curtain of shells and machine-gun fire made reinforcements or retreat impossible.

The *Légionnaires* dug in and throughout the night of the 16th until the afternoon following resisted all attacks. Then, covered with wounds and parched with thirst, the survivors surrendered.

The American squad when the first regiment moved north from the Champagne region early in May included Kenneth Weeks, of New Bedford; Paul Rockwell, of Atlanta; Paul Pavelka, of Madison, Conn.; Russell Kelly, of New York; Frank Musgrave, of New Orleans; Jack Janz, of Boston; Lawrence Scanlan, of Cedarhurst, L. I., John Smith, of Los Angeles; Neamorin, of Calcutta, a graduate of Oxford and a frequent visitor to America, and Madji Zennis, of Constantinople, formerly an interpreter for a New York importing house.

The squad was led by Corporal Didier, a gigantic Moor. All were volunteers for the war except Janz. Janz was the only American in the entire Legion that had seen African service, having been seven years in Morocco.

He was shot through the forehead while looking out of a trench toward the German lines shortly after the arrival of the regiment in the north.

During the fighting around La Targette and Neuville-St. Vaast on May 9th Janz was shot through the chest with a rifle ball. While he lay on the battlefield a shell exploded near him and badly lacerated his hips. Later he was carried off the field to a hospital.

Only 700 of 4,000 Left

After the fighting on May 9th, 10th and 11th the Legion was sent to the rear for reorganisation. Only 700 of the 4,000 who had gone into action answered the roll call.

In the attack of June 16th, which preceded by a terrific thirty-six-hour bombardment of the German lines, the legion occupied a position near Souchez and Cabaret Rouge.

The first line of German trenches was literally knocked to pieces by shell fire and easily taken. The advance on the second line was met by a stream of lead from rifles and machme guns. Whole sections of the attacking party were mowed down. Corporal Didier fell, his left arm literally shot off. Zennis's lower jaw was torn away. Neamorin fell with a ball through his abdomen.

Pavelka was the first of the American squad to reach the second line. He just got to the edge of a trench held by Bavarians when he was stabbed in the leg with a bayonet.

GERMANS THROW DOWN ARMS

By then the German trenches were filled with a yelling mass of Légionnaires *zouaves* and *tirailleurs*. Such of the Germans as could climbed out of the trenches and threw down their arms. They ran for the rear, the French in hot pursuit.

Pavelka took shelter in a German trench to bandage his wound. He was joined there by Kelly, who had been hit in the shoulder, mid Smith with a ball through his leg.

After a rest Pavelka suggested to his comrades that they crawl to the rear. Kelly and Smith were too weak. Pavelka made his way alone to a first aid ambulance.

The only American positively known to have been killed June 16th was Edwin Hall, of Chicago, who arrived at the front a few days before the battle and was placed in the machine gun section. It was his first time under fire and he exhibited great coolness and bravery. Hall's squad rushed up the machine guns to hold a captured position. The Germans counter attacked and killed the entire squad.

CHAPTER 9

Epilogue

It may interest the reader to know how the six Americans in the 15th *escouade* or squad have since fared, so the following brief statement is given.

Lawrence Scanlan, called Larney in the narrative, was severely wounded in his leg and foot June 16th. It was not until the following December that the last of the pieces of bullets were extracted from his leg. They were forwarded to his family near New York.

The wounds were so deep that in November, 1916, he was still an invalid, being in a hospital established by an American, Mrs. Fitzgerald, at Passy-par-Véron, France. In the summer of 1916 he was awarded the *Croix de Guerre* or Military Cross, the citation stating that it was awarded because he was a good and brave soldier and had been badly wounded. It was attached while he stood, aided by crutches. In writing of the ceremony he stated:

> I could not help thinking as I stood there that Russell should be standing beside me, and that we should be receiving our decorations together.

Paul Pavelka referred to in the letters as the "skipper," recovered from the bayonet wound he received June 16th, and returned to the front. He was in many severe engagements, and early in the year 1916 was transferred to the All-American aviation section. He rendered such brave service in this branch of the army around Verdun that he was made sergeant in September, 1916, and the following month was awarded the *Croix de Guerre* with its green and red ribbon.

Kniffin Yates Rockwell, who was in a hospital June 16th, suffering from the wound received May 9th, recovered and rejoined the Legion at the front. He was transferred to the All-American aviation section, and was so daring and successful that he became known as the Ace. General Joffre, in person, pinned upon him the *Médaille Militaire* with its yellow ribbon, for bringing down a Prussian two-seat aeroplane near Hartmannsweillerkopf, in May, 1916. On September 9th, 1916, he was officially credited with having brought down four Prussian aeroplanes. He was promoted to a lieutenancy. He was also awarded the *Croix de Guerre*.

On September 24th, 1916, he was shot down while defending a flotilla of bomb-dropping aeroplanes returning to the Verdun lines from an expedition into territories held by the Prussians. He suffered his fatal wound while above the town of Thann, and dropped into Alsatian territory, retaken from the Prussians. This was near the spot where he shot down his first adversary about April, 1916. He was on his way back to the air squadron's base where he would have been informed that he had been promoted from first sergeant to lieutenant. He was buried with full military honours, a regiment of French territorials and a battalion of Alpine *chasseurs* were the guard of honour.

Lieutenant Rockwell was from Atlanta, Georgia. He had been a cadet at the Virginia Military Institute, two classes ahead of Russell Kelly. Both were members of the Kappa Alpha fraternity.

Kenneth Weeks was reported as missing until November 25th, 1915, when his body was found between the lines of battle. It was learned that he had been killed June 16th, or 17th, and that his body had lain there for five months. He was buried in the military cemetery at Pylones near Mont St. Eloi.

He was from Boston, and had attended Harvard. He was an author of several books and possessed unusual literary ability.

The first reference to him in the above letters is in one from Verzenay in March, 1915, it states:

Another American was put in our squad; he is from Boston, has been in France five years, in the Legion five months and in the trenches three months. He is a fine fellow.

John Earl Fike of Wooster, Ohio, enlisted under the name of his grandfather, Captain John Smith, who had rendered distinguished services in our civil war. He and Russell Kelly disappeared during the battle, and have not been since heard from.

Many notices have been in the newspapers, tending to explain their absence, all of which on investigation proved incorrect.

The only authoritative information regarding either of them was that:

"Russell Kelly was seen in the second line of German trenches with a clean wound in his left shoulder that did not seem serious."

After sometime the names of these two were placed on the official list of "missing" and the French Minister of War notified their families that their names would he carried on that list until a search could be made in the internment camps of Germany.

The State Department at Washington had special inquiries made by the American ambassador at Berlin, and on January 3rd, 1916, Ambassador Gerard sent word from Berlin that their names were not reported among the prisoners of war in Germany.

The German War Office, the Imperial Foreign Office, the German Red Cross, as well as the International Red Cross at Geneva, Switzerland, reported that their names were not registered on any list in their possession.

On January 16th the *New York Sun* contained the following cable:

Paris, January 15th. Official news reached the Lyon depot today that Kenneth Weeks of Boston was killed on June 17th last year near Givenchy.
Official announcement also is made that John Earl Fike of Wooster, Ohio, was killed the same day. The death of Henry Farnsworth, another American in the Foreign Legion, reported on October 16th last, is officially confirmed.

On January 17th all the New York dailies contained the following cable:

Paris, January 16th. Five Americans attached to the Foreign Legion, whose names were included in the list of casualties at Givenchy on June 17th, are now officially reported as having been killed in action. They were Russell Kelly of New York, Harman Edwin Hall of Chicago, John Earl Fike of Wooster, Ohio, and Kenneth Weeks and Henry Farnsworth both of Boston.

In view of the discrepancy between these despatches, as well as the fact that seven months elapsed between the disappearance of Kelly and Fike and the publication of these so-called official notices, doubt was raised as to their authenticity, and the death of these two will not be conceded until the facts are disclosed upon which the conclusion of death is based. Besides, it is now known that the French War Office has not transferred the two names to the official list of dead.

JOHN EARL FIKE

The uncertainty of his death has been increased in the case of Russell Kelly, by information given by an English lady. She communicated with his family, and stated that in September of 1915 she received a letter from a relative in which he said he and two other English soldiers together with a French soldier, had been in hiding since the middle of the previous June, within the German lines, east of Souchez; and that French peasants had supplied them with clothing and food. It stated that the French soldier was an American named Kelly, and that he was badly wounded in the head. The letter had been surreptitiously passed through the lines.

The high character of the English lady, as well as many corroborating circumstances, have convinced the family of Russell Kelly of the truth of the statements; and there being no other American in the Foreign Legion named Kelly, they believe it refers to him, and that he is still alive.

An adjutant of the regiment sent word, in January, 1916, to Lyon, that he had seen Russell Kelly and two other prisoners in Belgium. He reported that Kelly had lost one of his legs and that he was careful not to disclose his American citizenship. The circumstances connected with this information show it to be consistent with the story of his being in hiding the previous September.

These rumours appear to be true but they cannot be satisfactorily verified.

It is known that the French prisoners in Belgium and northern France are not allowed to communicate in any way with the outside world, although prisoners in Germany are allowed to send and receive communications from relatives and friends.

It has been learned that these six Americans after receiving the warning of the opposition of Germany to Foreign *Légionnaires* who were not citizens of a country at war with Germany, discussed plans to be followed in the event of being taken prisoners.

They determined, if captured, to destroy all regimental marks on their uniforms, to throw away their army-books, and to assume fictitious names.

1914

November	3, left New York on steamship *Orcadian*.
"	19, reached Pauillac, France.
"	21, Saturday, docked at Bordeaux.
"	23, applied at recruiting station.
"	24, enlisted in the Foreign Legion.
"	26, began military training at Dépôt de Lyon.

1915

February	6, left barracks for the front.
"	8, arrived at Bouzy, near the front.
March	8, left Bouzy and same day arrived at Verzenay and entered first line trenches.
April	24, left Verzenay for region north of Arras.
"	28, reached Aubigny; again entered first line trenches.
May	9, Sunday, in the attack on La Targette and Neuville St. Vaast.
"	10, battle continued.
"	11, relieved from the captured position and returned with regiment to rear for reorganisation.
"	29, re-entered first line trenches.
June	16, in the attack on Cabaret Rouge near Souchez and at the taking of Hill No. 119.
"	18, reported as missing.
May	Still missing.

Is this military record, like the record of many another Legionary, forever closed; and does that youthful

Heart that once beat high for praise
Now feel that pulse no more?

CHAPTER 10

La Légion Étrangère

All the countries of the old world have "crack" military organizations famous for deeds of valour, many of which came into existence long before the time of our revolutionary war. In the United States, most large cities have at least one regiment with a record of which the civilians as well as the soldiers are justly proud. But all their histories and achievements pale before the extraordinary record, ancient formation and remarkable membership of France's famous corps, *la Légion étrangère*. That body is easily the most ancient, unique and widest known military organization in the world.

Here is a Legion numbering, before this war, eight thousand men, all of whom, except the officers, being aliens of the country for which they give up their lives. Very few of them are able to understand the language of the country, and very few become citizens of the country even after enlistment in its army.

They are not requested to enlist and when they do apply for admission they are told of the hardships to be encountered. If the applicant still insists he must wait until the following day before his application is considered.

Since the beginning of the present war many enlisted, no doubt, from love of France; but it is difficult to understand how this large membership was maintained prior to the war.

None enlisted for protection of their homes or families. Nor for glory as scarcely any Legionary has even become a general. Not for money; the pay is one cent a day, a wage the meanest outcast in the street would spurn with scorn. Not for comradeship; the ranks being recruited from the whole world are too cosmopolitan for lasting friendships.

Not for an easy life; for they were assigned, before this war, to duty in the unhealthy waste places of Africa and Asia. Answers to this riddle would be almost as diversified as the volunteers are numerous.

No weakling can be accepted, for it takes a good physique to stand the training necessary to develop a man to fight for his life and the country. For example it is part of the routine of the Legion for each company to march once a week, in full marching equipment, twenty-eight miles within ten hours.

Historians cannot agree as to when this Legion was first organized, but it is conceded that it was in existence in the time of Clovis who stands out in history as the founder of a new France, and with whose rule French history begins. He employed this very organisation in the year 486 when he defeated the last of the Roman power in northern Gaul, at Soissons, which city is still in existence and stands less than ten miles from the place where their equally courageous successors gave up their lives for that same France, but now a glorious republic, fourteen hundred and twenty-nine years later.

In our country we consider an institution that is one hundred years old as ancient, our government itself being in existence less than a century and a half, yet here is mi organisation that when Columbus discovered America, was a thousand years old.

Mercenaries, or troops who serve alien countries for pay, were used from the very earliest times. Thirteen thousand Greeks, fought in the year 401 B. C. under Cyrus, the Persian, against his brother Artaxerxes; and even the' all powerful Romans often availed themselves of the services of foreign soldiers.

The French always employed large numbers of mercenaries, and in the year 886 their king, Charles le Gros had a bodyguard of foreigners: an example followed by St. Louis in the year 1226. In the protracted wars between France and England in the thirteenth and fourteenth centuries these mercenaries formed the major part of both armies.

The last mercenaries used by England were twenty-two thousand Hessians hired from the *landgrave* Frederick II of Hesse-Casse, Prussia, and for whom they paid about £31,191,000 or $16,000,000, to assist in the war against the American colonies. These were the troops that Washington so decisively defeated at Trenton on Christmas night, 1776.

The Foreign Legion continued under all the French rulers, and Napoleon frequently acknowledged their great worth to him.

After the Napoleonic wars the Legion was known as The Royal Foreign Legion. In 1831 a new law was enacted reorganizing the Legion and establishing its headquarters in Algeria. In 1835 the Legion was the subject of one of the most remarkable transactions in history; it was sold by King Louis Philippe to Queen Maria Christina of Spain for a sum equal to about one hundred and seventeen thousand dollars, being the estimated value of its arms, uniforms and equipment.

The Legion proceeded to Spain landing at Tarragona, four thousand strong; it fought valiantly for four years in the first Carlist war, and when that war ended in the early part of 1839 only five hundred *Légionnaires* survived.

Within a few weeks after the old Legion landed in Spain, a new Legion was organized by France and sent to Algeria, where it did most effective work.

In the Crimea war the Legion was part of Canrobert's division at the battle of the Alma; and during the siege of Sevastopol it was repeatedly mentioned in reports for its brave and successful efforts. In this campaign the Legion lost eighteen hundred officers and men, and as a reward for their gallantry the emperor gave the *Légionnaires* the right to become French citizens should they desire to.

The Legion was part of Maximilian's forces in Mexico and on April 30th, 1863, near the village of Camaron, a detachment of three officers and Sixty-five *Légionnaires* held at bay two thousand Mexican cavalry for ten hours, when the survivors numbering only twenty were captured. As a reward the word "Camaron" is inscribed on the colours of the First Regiment.

Four thousand two hundred and thirty-seven officers and men of the Legion died in Mexico.

In the Franco-Prussian war of 1870 the Legion performed remarkable services as a rear guard, to cover the retreat of the French army.

The Legion in time of peace consists of two regiments, the *Premier* or First, and *Deuxième* or Second, they being kept separate and distinct. The headquarters of the First Regiment is at Sidi-Bel-Abbés which is in the north-western part of Algeria, forty-eight miles inland by rail from Oran, a port on the Mediterranean. The headquarters of the Second Regiment is at Saida, also in Algeria,

The First Regiment has thereat distinction of having had its flag decorated with the Cross of the Legion of Honour, only ten regiments of the three hundred and odd composing all branches of the French army having this great honour. It is the boast of its soldiers that "the Legion of Honour dwells with us." This regiment's flag carries the motto

"*Honneur et Discipline*";

The flags in the other regiments of the French army bear the motto

"*Honneur et Patrie.*"

So these wanderers from all countries, after enlistment are without a country.

At the beginning of the present war these two regiments were mobilized, and there being a large number of volunteers, each regiment was divided into four regiments and designated as *régiments de Marche*, or marching regiments. Each *régiment de Marche* was divided into four battalions, being known as A, B, C and D; a battalion consisted of four companies; each company of four sections; each section of four squads, and there were sixteen men to a squad. This arrangement accounts for four thousand and ninety-six men, and as there were additional officers and *attachés*, a full *Régiment de Marche* was frequently composed of as many as four thousand four hundred men.

The four *régiments de Marche* of the First *Régiment étrangère* were, therefore, about seventeen thousand strong.

The Second *Régiment étrangère* was, in the same way, divided into four *régiments de Marche*, and was of the same numerical strength as the First *Régiment étrangère*. Hence, the Foreign Legion in April and May, 1915, when its ranks were full, consisted of about thirty-four thousand troops.

The First *Régiment de Marche* of the First *Régiment étrangère* was composed mostly of Garibaldians, the second of Swedes, Spaniards, Russians, Canadians, English, Americans, and others, while the third and fourth were mostly Greeks.

The designation of Russell A. Kelly was as follows:

Soldat KELLY. RusseU. No. 24641
1 *Régiment étrangère*
2 Régiment de Marche Battalion B
2 *Compagnie*
4 Section
15 *Escouade*

The *Légionnaires* who survived the battle of June 16th, 1915, being very few in number, were assigned some weeks later to the Second foreign regiment, then located in the Champagne district, to the east of Rheims.

On September 25th, that regiment took part in a very severe attack on the German lines between Souain and Perthes-le-Hurlus, about twenty-seven miles from Rheims. This attack continued on the 26th, 27th and 28th and was entirely successful, for they finally captured the redoubt of Bois Sabot, but at the cost of more than half of the regiment. This engagement is now designated as the Battle of Champagne, and is considered one of the most important battles of the war.

The Legion, after being recruited and generally strengthened, next took part in the very severe fighting in December at Hartmanns-weilerkopf in the Vosges.

It did exceptional work in the severe battles around Verdun in February and March. The— following despatch was sent from Paris March 7th, 1916:

> The unanimous French military opinion is that the recapture of Douaumont by the French infantry line, the Foreign Legion and chasseurs, on Feb. 26th, was one of the finest feats in military annals and equal to Gen. Galliéni's famous charge at Sedan in 1870.

In the summer of 1916 the French Government revived the ancient *fourragère* decoration; this consists of a braided cord about 34 inches long, terminating in an aiguillette; one end is fastened on the soldier's left shoulder, and then extended under his left arm and fastened on his left breast so that the aiguillette hangs below this second fastening.

It is not awarded for individual merit, but is conferred on a military unit, as a section, company, battalion, or sometimes an entire regiment; it is a reward for two distinct citations for unusual bravery or heroism.

Almost the first award made was to the entire Second *Régiment de Marche* of the First Foreign Regiment. The two citations entitling the regiment to this revived decoration were, first, for its extraordinary work during the Battle of Artois, which began May 9th and ended June 19th, 1915; and second, for equally meritorious and successful action during the battle of Champagne, which took place from September 20th to October 17th, 1915.

For several years prior to the present war, the Germans very bitterly attacked the French Foreign Legion by articles in their newspapers and magazines, as well as pictures in their moving picture shows and songs in their *café* concerts. One very violent attack was a play entitled, *The Hypocrite*, which was first produced February 24th, 1914, at the Künstler Theatre, Berlin.

In a ray of green light a legionary advanced toward the front of the stage with a sign inscribed. "We are the *Légionnaires* of Africa" written in French; it continued in German, "All that you behold here is strictly true; we show you what we suffer and how we die."

The play was received with great applause, although the critic of the *Berliner Tageblait* had the fairness to write, "This drama of the Legion is a sluggish and untimely melody of the boulevard."

Germany's arguments against the Legion were summarized in the Spring of 1914 as follows, *viz.*:

First. They deny the right of a modern, state to have recourse for its defence to the services of foreign subjects and they say they have been confirmed in this by the fact that all states, except France, have successively renounced the employment of foreign soldiers.

Second. That the contract on enlistment is harsh as the duration of the services is too long, the pay is insufficient and the service imposed is excessive.

Third. That France takes advantage of the wretchedness of the applicants and secures their enlistment while they are in ignorance of the severity of the service.

Fourth. That recruiting is carried on by crimps who abuse their victims by getting them drunk and by false promises, and it results in forming a scandalous mixture of starving men, adventurers and bandits, devoted to drunkenness and the most infamous morals.

Fifth. That it is applicable to minors, recruits being taken at the age of eighteen years.

Sixth. That Germany has, more than any other country, the right to occupy itself with that which is going on in the Legion, by reason of the great number of its subjects who serve here.

Mr. Gaston Moch issued a book in Paris in 1914, before the war, entitled *The Question of the Foreign Legion*, in which he fully discusses these arguments from the French side. The Foreign Legion is, therefore, acknowledged to be the last of the mercenaries, a connecting link between the present day and the days before the beginning of the Christian era.

A Soldier of the Legion

THE SOLDIER

Contents

.

Preface

When Sergeant Morlae turned up at the Atlantic office and, with his head cocked on one side, remarked ingratiatingly, "I'm told this is the highest-toned office in the United States," there was nothing to do but to assure him he was right and to make him quite comfortable while he told his wonderful story. That story, however, was not told consecutively, but in chapters as his crowding recollections responded to the questions of his interlocutor. It was a story, too, which could not be told at a sitting, and it was not until the evening of the second day that Sergeant Morlae recounted the exploit which won the *Croix de Guerre* pinned to his chest—a cross which he said, with the sole touch of personal pride noticed in three days passed largely in his company, had above it not the copper but the silver clasp.

Sergeant Morlae is a Dirk Hatteraick of a man to look at, and the education of that beloved pirate was no more rugged than his own. His father was a Frenchman born who had seen service in '70 and won a captain's commission in the "Terrible Year." After the war, Morlae, senior, settled in this country and his son was born in California. As young Morlae grew up, finding the family business of contracting on a small scale somewhat circumscribed, he sought more hazardous employment in active service in the Philippines and in more than one civilian "scrap" in Mexico.

It was good training. August, 1914, found him again in Los Angeles. For two days his French blood mounted as he read the newspapers, and on the morning of August 3 he packed his grip and started for Paris to enlist in the Legion. Since he had already seen service, he was soon made a corporal and later a sergeant. Morlae, says a letter from a Harvard graduate who served under him in those days, was "an excellent soldier," "a strong, efficient, ambitious man," though, as the reader of this and letters from other Legionaries may infer, he was neither sentimental in his methods nor supersensitive with his men. Maintaining discipline in so motley a crew as the Legion is rather a rasping process, and Sergeant Morlae was born disqualified for diplomatic service. Future reunions of *La Légion* are likely to lack the sweet placidity which wraps the Grand Army of the Republic on the anniversaries of Chancellorsville and Gettysburg.

But to the story. The things that war is are not often told except in generalization or in words of fanciful rhetoric. It would be hard to find elsewhere, crammed into a brief narrative, so much of the sense of actuality—that realism made perfect which even readers who have known no such experience feel instinctively is true. Yet the story is not made of horror. The essence of its life is the spirit that delights in peril. The *Soldier of the Legion* has in it that spinal thrill which has electrified great tales of battle since blood was first let and ink spilled to celebrate it.

Ellery Sedgwick.

CHAPTER 1

The Foreign Legion

One day during the latter part of August, 1915, my regiment, the *2ᵐᵉ Étranger* (Foreign Legion), passed in review before the President of the French Republic and the commander-in-chief of her armies, General Joffre. On that day, after twelve months of fighting, the regiment was presented by President Poincare with a battle-flag. The occasion marked the admission of the *Légion Étrangerè* to equal footing with the regiments of the line. Two months later—it was October 28—the remnants of this regiment were paraded through the streets of Paris, and, with all military honours, this same battle-flag was taken across the Seine to the *Hôtel des Invalides*. There it was decorated with the cross of the Legion of Honour, and, with reverent ceremony, was placed between the flag of the *cuirassiers* who died at Reichshofen and the equally famous standard which the Garibaldians bore in 1870-71. The flag lives on. The regiment has ceased to exist.

On the battlefield of La Champagne, from Souain to the Ferme Navarin, from Somme Py to the Butte de Souain, the ground is thickly studded with low wooden crosses and plain pine boards marked with the Mohammedan crescent and star. Beside the crosses you see bayonets thrust into the ground, and dangling from their cross-bars little metal disks which months ago served their purpose in identifying the dead and now mark their graves. Many mounds bear no mark at all. On others again you see a dozen helmets laid in rows, to mark the companionship of the dead below in a common grave. It is there you will find the Legion.

Of the Legion I can tell you at first-hand. It is a story of adventurers, of criminals, of fugitives from justice. Some of them are drunkards, some thieves, and some with the mark of Cain upon them find others to keep them company. They are men I know the worst of. And yet I

95

am proud of them—proud of having been one of them; very proud of having commanded some of them.

It is all natural enough. Most men who had come to know them as I have would feel as I do. You must reckon the good with the evil. You must remember their comradeship, their *esprit de corps*, their pathetic eagerness to serve France, the sole country which has offered them asylum, the country which has shown them confidence, mothered them, and placed them on an equal footing with her own sons. These things mean something to a man who has led the life of an outcast, and the *Légionnaires* have proved their loyalty many times over. At Arras there are more than four hundred kilometres of trench-line which they have restored to France. The Legion has always boasted that it never shows its back, and the Legion has made good.

In my own section there were men of all races and all nationalities. There were Russians and Turks, an Annamite and a Hindu. There were Frenchmen from God knows where. There was a German, God only knows why. There were Bulgars, Serbs, Greeks, negroes, an Italian, and a Fiji Islander fresh from an Oxford education,—a silent man of whom it was whispered that he had once been an archbishop,—three Arabians, and a handful of Americans who cared little for the quiet life. As Bur-bek-kar, the Arabian bugler, used to say in his bad French, "*Ceux sont le ra-ta international*"—"They're the international stew."

Many of the men I came to know well. The Italian, Conti, had been a professional bicycle-thief who had slipped quietly into the Legion when things got too hot for him. When he was killed in Champagne he was serving his second enlistment. Doumergue, a Frenchman who was a particularly good type of soldier, had absconded from Paris with his employer's money and had found life in the Legion necessary to his comfort. A striking figure with a black complexion was Voronoff, a Russian prince whose precise antecedents were unknown to his mates. Pala was a Parisian "Apache" and looked the part. Every man had left a past behind him. But the Americans in the Legion were of a different type. Some of us who volunteered for the war loved fighting, and some of us loved France. I was fond of both.

But even the Americans were not all of one stripe. J. J. Casey had been a newspaper artist, and Bob Scanlon, a burly negro, an artist with his fist in the squared ring. Alan Seeger had something of the poet in him. Dennis Dowd was a lawyer; Edwin Bouligny a lovable adventurer. There was D. W. King, the sprig of a well-known family. William Thaw, of Pittsburg, started with us, though he joined the Flying Corps later on. Then there were James Bach, of New York; B. S. Hall, who hailed from Kentucky; Professor Ohlinger, of Columbia; Phelizot, who had shot enough big game in Africa to feed the regiment. There were Delpeuch, and Capdeville, and little Tinkard, from New York. Bob Soubiron came, I imagine, from the United States in general, for he had been a professional automobile racer. The Rockwell brothers, journalists, signed on from Georgia; and last, though far from least, was Friedrich Wilhelm Zinn, from Battle Creek, Michigan.

The rest of the section were old-time *Légionnaires*, most of them serving their second enlistment of five years, and some their third. All these were seasoned soldiers, veterans of many battles in Algiers and Morocco. My section—complete—numbered sixty. Twelve of us survive, and of these there are several still in the hospital recovering from wounds. Zinn and Tinkard lie there with bullets in their breasts; Dowd, with his right arm nearly severed; Soubiron, shot in the leg; Bouligny, with a ball in his stomach. But Bouligny, like many another, is an old hand in the hospital. He has been there twice before with metal to be cut out. Several others lie totally incapacitated from wounds, and more than half of the section rests quietly along the route of the regiment. Seven of them are buried at Craonne; two more at Ferme Alger, near Rheims. Eighteen of them I saw buried myself in Champagne.

That is the record of the first section of Company I. Section III, on the night of the first day's fighting in Champagne, mustered eight men out of the forty-two who had fallen into line that morning. Section IV lost that day more than half of its effectives. Section II lost seventeen out of thirty-eight. War did its work thoroughly with the Legion. We had the place of honour in the attack, and we paid for it.

CHAPTER 2

Preparations

Two days before the forward movement began, we were informed by our captain of the day and hour set for the attack. We were told the exact number of field-pieces and heavy guns which would support us and the number of shells to be fired by each piece. Our artillery had orders to place four shells per metre per minute along the length of the German lines. Our captain gave us also very exact information regarding the number of German batteries opposed to us. He even told us the regimental numbers of the Prussian and Saxon regiments which were opposite our line. From him we learned also that along the whole length of our first row of trenches steps had been cut into the front bank in order to enable us to mount it without delay, and that our own barbed-wire entanglements, which were immediately in front of this trench, had been pierced by lanes cut through every two metres, so that we might advance without the slightest hindrance.

On the night of September 23, the commissioned officers, including the colonel of the regiment, entered the front lines of trenches, and with stakes marked the front to be occupied by our regiment during the attack. It was like an arrangement for a race. Starting from the road leading from Souain to Vouziers, the officers, after marking the spot with a big stake, paced fifteen hundred metres to the eastward and there marked the extreme right of the regiment's position by a second stake. Midway between these two a third was placed. From the road to the stake, the seven hundred and fifty metres marked the terrain for Battalion C. The other seven hundred and fifty metres bearing to the left were assigned to Battalion D. Just one hundred metres behind these two battalions a line was designated for Battalion E, which was to move up in support.

My own company formed the front line of the extreme left flank of the regiment. Our left was to rest on the highroad and our front was to run from that to a stake marking a precise frontage of two hundred metres. From these stakes, which marked the ends of our line, we were ordered to take a course due north, sighting our direction by trees and natural objects several kilometres in the rear of the German lines. These were to serve us for guides during the advance. After all these matters had been explained to us at length, other details were taken up with the engineers, who were shown piles of bridging, ready made in sections of planking so that they might be readily placed over the German trenches and thus permit our guns and supply-wagons to cross quickly in the wake of our advance.

The detail was infinite, but everything was foreseen. Twelve men from each company were furnished with long knives and grenades. Upon these "trench-cleaners," as we called them, fell the task of entering the German trenches and caves and bomb-proofs, and disposing of such of the enemy as were still hidden therein after we had stormed the trench and passed on to the other side. All extra shoes, all clothing and blankets were turned in to the quartermaster, and each man was provided with a second canteen of water, two days of "iron rations," and one hundred and thirty rounds additional, making two hundred and fifty cartridges per man. The gas-masks and mouth-pads were ready; emergency dressings were inspected, and each man ordered to put on clean underwear and shirts to prevent possible infection of the wounds.

One hour before the time set for the advance, we passed the final inspection and deposited our last letters with the regimental postmaster. Those letters meant a good deal to all of us and they were in our minds during the long wait that followed. One man suddenly began to intone the "*Marseillaise*." Soon every man joined in singing. It was a very Anthem of Victory. We were ready, eager, and confident: for us to-morrow held but one chance—Victory.

CHAPTER 3

On the Move

Slowly the column swung out of camp, and slowly and silently, without a spoken word of command, it changed its direction to the right and straightened out its length upon the road leading to the trenches. It was 10 p.m. precisely by my watch. The night was quite clear, and we could see, to right and to left, moving columns marching parallel to ours. One, though there was not quite light enough to tell which, was our sister regiment, the *1er Régiment Étranger*. The other, as I knew, was the *8me Zouaves*. The three columns marched at the same gait. It was like a funeral march, slow and very quiet. There was no singing and shouting; none of the usual badinage. Even the officers were silent. They were all on foot, marching like the rest of us. We knew there would be no use for horses tomorrow.

Tomorrow was the day fixed for the grand attack. There was not a man in the ranks who did not know that tomorrow, at 9.15, was the time set. Every man, I suppose, wondered whether he would do or whether he would die. I wondered myself.

I did not really think I should die. Yet I had arranged my earthly affairs. "One can never tell," as the French soldier says with a shrug. I had written to my friends at home. I had named the men in my company to whom I wished to leave my personal belongings. Sergeant Velte was to have my Parabellum pistol; Casey my prismatics; Birchler my money-belt and its contents; while Sergeant Jovert was booked for my watch and compass. Yet, in the back of my mind, I smiled at my own forethought. I *knew* that I should come out alive. I recalled to myself the numerous times that I had been in imminent peril in the Philippines, in Mexico, and during the thirteen months of this war. I could remember time and again when men were killed on each side of me and I escaped unscratched. Take the affair of Papoin, Joly,

As they swing into column the night before the 25th of September

and Bob Scanlon. We were standing together so near that we could have clasped hands. Papoin was killed, Joly was severely wounded, and Scanlon was hit in the ankle—all by the same shell. The fragments which killed and wounded the first two passed on one side of me, while the piece of iron that bit Bob went close by my other side. Yet I was untouched! Again, take the last patrol. When I was out of cover, the Germans shot at me from a range of ten metres—and missed! I felt certain that my day was not tomorrow.

Just the same, I was glad that my affairs were arranged, and it gave me a sense of conscious satisfaction to think that my comrades would have something to remember me by. There is always the chance of something unforeseen happening.

The pace was accelerating. The strain was beginning to wear off. From right and left there came a steady murmur of low talk. In our own column men were beginning to chaff each other. I could distinctly hear Soubiron describing in picturesque detail to Capdeveille how he, Capdeveille, would look, gracefully draped over the German barbed wire; and I could hear Capdeveille's heated response that he would live long enough to spit upon Soubiron's grave; and I smiled to myself. The moment of depression and self-communication had passed. The men had found themselves and were beginning their usual chaffing. And yet, in all their chatter there seemed to be an unusually sharp note. The jokes all had an edge to them. References to one another's death were common, and good wishes for one another's partial dismemberment excited only laughter. Just behind me I heard King express the hope that if he lost an arm or a leg he would at least get the *médaille militaire* in exchange. By way of comfort, his chum, Dowd, remarked that, whether he got the medal or not, he was very sure of getting a permit to beg on the street-corners.

From personal bickerings we passed on to a discussion of the Germans and German methods of making war. We talked on the finer points of hand-grenades, poison gas, flame-projectors, vitriol bombs, and explosive bullets. Everybody seemed to take particular pleasure in describing the horrible wounds caused by the different weapons. Each man embroidered upon the tales the others told.

We were marching into hell. If you judged them by their conversation, these men must have been brutes at heart, worse than any "Apache"; and yet of those around me several were university graduates; one was a lawyer; two were clerks; one a poet of standing; one an actor; and there were several men of leisure, Americans almost all of them.

The talk finally settled upon the Germans. Many and ingenious were the forms of torture invented upon the spur of the moment for the benefit of the "Boches." "Hanging is too good for them," said Scanlon. After a long discussion, scalping alive seemed the most satisfactory to the crowd.

It had come to be 11 p.m. We were at the mouth of the communicating trench and entering it, one by one. Every so often, short transverse trenches opened up to right and left, each one crammed full of soldiers. Talking and laughing stopped. We continued marching along the trench, kilometre after kilometre, in utter silence. As we moved forward, the lateral trenches became more numerous. Every fifteen to eighteen feet we came to one running from right to left, and each was filled with troops, their arms grounded. As we filed slowly by, they looked at us enviously. It was amusing to see how curious they looked, and to watch their whispering as we passed. Why should we precede them in attack?

"Who are you?" several men asked.

"*La Légion.*"

"A-a-ah, *la Légion!* That explains it"

Our right to the front rank seemed to he acknowledged. It did every man of us good.

We debouched from the trench into the street of a village. It was Souain. Houses, or ghosts of houses, walled us in on each side. Through the windows and the irregular shell-holes in the walls, the stars twinkled; while through a huge gap in the upper storey of one of the houses I caught a glimpse of the moon, over my right shoulder. Lucky omen! "I'll come through all right," I repeated to myself, and rapped with my knuckle upon the rifle-stock, lest the luck break.

Not one house in the village was left standing—only bare walls. Near the end of the street, in the midst of chaos, we passed a windmill. The gaunt steel frame still stood. I could see the black rents in the mill and the great arms where the shrapnel had done its work; but still the wheel turned, slowly, creaking round and round, with its shrill metal scream.

The column turned to the left and again disappeared in a trench. After a short distance we turned to the right, then once more to the left, then on, and finally, not unwillingly, we came to a rest. We did not have to be told that we were now in the front line, for through the rifle-ports we could see the French shells bursting ahead of us like

Fourth-of-July rockets.

The artillery had the range perfectly, and the shells, little and big, plumped with pleasing regularity into the German trenches. The din was indescribable—almost intolerable. Forty, even fifty, shells per minute were falling into a space about a single kilometre square. The explosions sounded almost continuous, and the return fire of the Germans seemed almost continuous. Only the great ten-inch long-range Teuton guns continued to respond effectively.

We looked at the show for a while, and then lay down in the trench. Every man used his knapsack for a pillow and tried to snatch a few hours' sleep. It was not a particularly good place for a nervous sleeper, but we were healthy and pretty tired.

The next morning, at 8 a.m., hot coffee was passed round, and we breakfasted on sardines, cheese, and bread, with the coffee to wash it down. At 9 the command passed down the line, "Every man ready!" Up went the knapsack on every man's back, and, rifle in hand, we filed along the trench.

The cannonading seemed to increase in intensity. From the low places in the parapet we caught glimpses of barbed wire which would glisten in occasional flashes of light. Our own we could plainly see, and a little farther beyond was the German wire.

Suddenly, at the sound of a whistle, we halted. The command, "*Baïonnette au canon!*" passed down the section. A drawn-out rattle followed, and the bayonets were fixed. Then the whistle sounded again. This time twice. We adjusted our straps. Each man took a look at his neighbour's equipment. I turned and shook hands with the fellows next to me. They were grinning, and I felt my own nerves a-quiver as we waited for the signal.

Waiting seemed an eternity. As we stood there a shell burst close to our left. A moment later it was whispered along the line that an adjutant and five men bad gone down.

What were we waiting for? I glanced at my watch. It was 9.15 exactly. The Germans evidently had the range. Two more shells burst close to the same place. We inquired curiously who was hit this time. Our response was two whistles. That was our signal. I felt my jaws clenching, and the man next to me looked white. It was only for a second. Then every one of us rushed at the trench wall, each and every man struggling to be the first out of the trench. In a moment we had clambered up and out. We slid over the parapet, wormed our way through gaps in the wire, formed in line, and, at the command, moved forward at march-step straight toward the German wire.

The world became a roaring hell. Shell after shell burst near us, sometimes right among us; and, as we moved forward at the double-quick, men fell right and left. We could hear the subdued rattling of the *mitrailleuses* and the roar of volley fire, but, above it all, I could hear with almost startling distinctness the words of the captain, shouting in his clear, high voice, "*En avant! Vive la France!*"

CHAPTER 4

Advance to Ferme Navarin

As we marched forward toward our goal, huge geysers of dust spouted into the air, rising behind our backs from the rows of "75's" supporting us. In front the fire-curtain outlined the whole length of the enemy's line with a neatness and accuracy that struck me with wonder, as the flames burst through the pall of smoke and dust around us. Above, all was blackness, but at its lower edge the curtain was fringed with red and green flames, marking the explosion of the shells directly over the ditch and parapet in front of us. The low-flying clouds mingled with the smoke-curtain, so that the whole brightness of the day was obscured. Out of the blackness fell a trickling rain of pieces of metal, lumps of earth, knapsacks, rifles, cartridges, and fragments of human flesh. We went on steadily, nearer and nearer. Now we seemed very close to the wall of shells streaming from our own guns, curving just above us, and dropping into the trenches in front. The effect was terrific. I almost braced myself against the rocking of the earth, like a sailor's instinctive gait in stormy weather.

In a single spot immediately in front of us, not over ten metres in length, I counted twelve shells bursting so fast that I could not count them without missing other explosions. The scene was horrible and terrifying. Across the wall of our own fire poured shell after shell from the enemy, tearing through our ranks. From overhead the shrapnel seemed to come down in sheets, and from behind the stinking, blinding curtain came volleys of steel-jacketed bullets, their whine unheard and their effect almost unnoticed.

I think we moved forward simply from habit. With me it was like a dream as we went on, ever on. Here and there men dropped, the ranks closing automatically. Of a sudden our own fire-curtain lifted. In a moment it had ceased to bar our way and jumped like a living thing to the next line of the enemy. We could see the trenches in front of us now, quite clear of fire, but flattened almost beyond recognition. The defenders were either killed or demoralized. Calmly, almost stupidly, we parried or thrust with the bayonet at those who barred our way. Without a backward glance we leaped the ditch and went on straight forward toward the next trench, marked in glowing outline by our fire. I remember now how the men looked. Their eyes had a wild, unseeing look in them. Everybody was gazing ahead, trying to pierce the awful curtain which cut us off from all sight of the enemy. Always the black pall smoking and burning appeared ahead—just ahead of us—hiding everything we wanted to see. The drama was played again and again. Each time, as we approached so close that fragments of our own shells occasionally struck a leading file, the curtain lifted as by magic, jumped the intervening metres, and descended upon the enemy's trench farther on. The ranges were perfect. We followed blindly—sometimes at a walk, sometimes at a dog-trot, and, when close to our goal, on the dead run. You could not hear a word in that pandemonium. All commands were given by example or by gesture. When our captain lay down, we knew our orders were to lie down too. When he waved to the right, to the right we swerved; if to the left, we turned to the left. A sweeping gesture, with an arm extended, first up, then down meant, "Halt! Lie down!" From down up, it meant, "Rise!" When his hand was thrust swiftly forward, we knew he was shouting, "*En avant!*" and when he waved his hand in a circle above his head, we broke into the double-quick.

Three times on our way to the second trench, the captain dropped and we after him. Then three short, quick rushes by the companies and a final dash as the curtain of shells lifted and dropped farther away. Then a hand-to-hand struggle, short and very bloody, some using their bayonets, others clubbing their rifles and grenades. A minute or two, and the trench was ours. The earthen fortress, so strong that the Germans had boasted that it could be held by a janitor and two washerwomen, was in the hands of the Legion.

As we swept on, the trench-cleaners entered the trench behind and began setting things to rights. Far down, six to eight metres below the surface, they found an underground city. Long tunnels, with chambers opening to right and left; bedrooms, furnished with bedsteads, washstands, tables, and chairs; elaborate mess-rooms, some fitted with pianos and phonographs. There were kitchens, too, and even bathrooms. So complex was the labyrinth that three days after the attack

AMERICANS IN THE FOREIGN LEGION
Showing types of hand-grenades

Germans were found stowed away in the lateral galleries. The passages were choked with dead. Hundreds of Germans who had survived the bombardment were torn to pieces deep beneath the ground by French hand-grenades, and buried where they lay. In rifles, munitions, and equipment the booty was immense.

We left the subterranean combat raging underneath us and continued on. As we passed over the main trench, we were enfiladed by cannon placed in armoured turrets at the end of each section of trench. The danger was formidable, but it, too, had been foreseen. In a few moments these guns were silenced by hand-grenades shoved point-blank through the gun-ports. Just then, I remember, I looked back and saw Pala down on his hands and knees. I turned and ran over to help him up. He was quite dead, killed in the act of rising from the ground. His grotesque posture struck me at the time as funny, and I could not help smiling. I suppose I was nervous.

Our line was wearing thin. Halfway to the third trench we were reinforced by Battalion E coming from behind. The ground in our rear was covered with our men.

All at once came a change. The German artillery in front ceased firing, and the next second we saw the reason why. In the trench ahead, the German troops in black masses were pouring out and advancing toward us at a trot. Was it a counter-attack? "*Tant mieux,*" said a man near me; another, of a different race, said, "We'll show them!" Then as suddenly our own artillery ceased firing, and the mystery became plain. The Germans were approaching in columns of fours, officers to the front, hands held in the air, and, as they came closer, we could distinguish the steady cry, "*Kameraden! Kameraden!*"

They were surrendering. How we went at our work! Out flew our knives, and, in less time than it takes to tell it, we had mingled among the prisoners, slicing off their trousers buttons, cutting off suspenders, and hacking through belts. All the war shoes had their laces cut, according to the regulations laid down in the last French "*Manual,*" and thus, slopping along, hands helplessly in their breeches pockets to keep their trousers from falling round their ankles, shuffling their feet to keep their boots on, the huge column of prisoners was sent to the rear with a few soldiers to direct rather than to guard them. There was no fight left in them now. A terror-stricken group; some of them, temporarily at least, half insane.

As the Germans left the trenches, their artillery had paused, thinking it a counter-attack. Now, as file after file was escorted to the rear and it became apparent to their rear lines that the men had surrendered, the German artillery saw its mistake and opened up again furiously at the dark masses of defenceless prisoners. We, too, were subjected to a terrific fire. Six shells landed at the same instant in almost the same place, and within a few minutes Section III of our company had almost disappeared. I lost two of my own section, Casey and Leguen, both severely wounded in the leg. I counted fourteen men of my command still on their feet. The company seemed to have shrunk two thirds. A few minutes later, we entered the trench lately evacuated by the Prussians and left it by a very deep communication trench which we knew led to our destination, Ferme Navarin. Just at the entrance we passed signboards, marked in big letters with black paint, *Schützengraben Spandau.*

This trench ran zigzag, in the general direction north and south. In many places it was filled level with dirt and rocks kicked in by our big shells. From the mass of debris hands and legs were sticking stiffly out at grotesque angles. In one place, the heads of two men showed above the loose brown earth. Here and there, men were sitting, their backs against the wall of the trench, quite dead, with not a wound showing. In one deep crater, excavated by our 320-millimetres, lay five Saxons, side by side, in the pit where they had sought refuge, killed by the bursting of a single shell. One, a man of about twenty-three years of age, lay on his back, his legs tensely doubled, elbows thrust back into the ground, and fingers dug into the palms; eyes staring in terror and mouth wide open. I could not help carrying the picture of fear away with me, and I thought to myself "that man died a coward." Just alongside of him, resting on his left side, lay a blond giant stretched out easily, almost graceful in death. His two hands were laid together, palm to palm, in prayer. Between them was a photograph. The look upon his face was calm and peaceful. The contrast of his figure with his neighbour's struck me. I noticed that a paper protruded from his partly opened blouse, and, picking it up, I read the heading, "*Ein' Feste Burg ist Unser Gott.*" It was a two-leaved tract. I drew a blanket over him and followed my section.

The trench we marched in wound along in the shelter of a little ridge crowned with scrubby pines. Here the German shells bothered us but little. We were out of sight of their observation posts, and, consequently, their fire was uncontrolled and no longer effective. On we went. At every other step our feet pressed down upon soldiers' corpses, lying indiscriminately one on top of the other, sometimes almost filling the trench. I brushed against one who sat braced against the side of the trench, the chin resting upon folded arms naturally—yet quite dead. It was through this trench that the Germans had tried to rush reinforcements into the threatened position, and here the men were slaughtered, without a chance to go back or forward. Hemmed in by shells in both front and rear, many hundreds had climbed into the open and tried to escape over the fields toward the pine forest, only to be mown down as they ran. For hundreds of metres continuously my feet, as I trudged along, did not touch the ground. In many of the bodies life was not yet extinct, but we had to leave them for the Red Cross men. We had our orders. No delay was possible, and, at any rate, our minds were clogged with our own work ahead.

Making such time as we could, we finally arrived at the summit of the little ridge. Then we left the cover of the trench, formed in Indian file, fifty metres between sections, and, at the signal, moved forward swiftly and in order.

It was a pretty bit of tactics and executed with a dispatch and neatness hardly equalled on the drill-ground. The first files of the sections were abreast, while the men fell in, one close behind the other; and so we crossed the ridge, offering the smallest possible target to the enemy's guns. Before us and a little to our left was the Ferme Navarin, our goal. As we descended the slope, we were greeted by a new hail of iron. Shells upon shells, fired singly, by pairs, by salvos, from six-gun batteries, crashed and exploded around us.

We increased the pace to a run and arrived out of breath abreast of immense pits dynamited out of the ground by prodigious explosions. Embedded in them we could see three enemy howitzers, but not a living German was left. All had disappeared.

We entered the pits and rested for a space. After a moment we crawled up the side of the pit and peeked over the edge. There I could see Doumergue stretched on the ground. He was lying on his back, his shoulders and head supported by his knapsack. His right leg was doubled under him, and I could see that he had been struck down in the act of running. As I watched, he strained weakly to roll himself sideways and free his leg. Slowly, spasmodically, his leg moved. Very, very slowly the foot dragged itself along the ground, and finally the limb was stretched alongside the other. Then I saw his rough, wan face assume a look of satisfaction. His eyes closed. A sigh passed between his lips, and Doumergue had gone with the rest.

As we waited there, the mood of the men seemed to change. Their spirits began to rise. One jest started another, and soon we were all laughing at the memory of the German prisoners marching to the rear, holding up their trousers with both hands. Some of the men had taken the welcome opportunity of searching the prisoners while cutting their suspenders, and most of them were now puffing German cigarettes. One of them, Haeffle, offered me a piece of K. K. bread, [1] black as ink. I declined with thanks, for I didn't like the looks of it. In the relaxation of the moment, nobody paid any attention to the shells falling outside the little open shelter, until Capdeveille proposed to crawl inside one of the German howitzers for security. Alas, he was too fat, and stuck! I myself hoped rather strongly that no shell would enter one of these pits in which the company had found shelter, because I knew there were several thousand rounds of ammunition piled near each piece hidden under the dirt, and an explosion might make it hot for us.

As we sat there, smoking and chatting, Delpeuch, the *homme des liaisons*, as he is called, of the company, slid over the edge of the hollow and brought with him the order to leave the pit in single file and to descend to the bottom of the incline, in line with some trees which he pointed out to us. There we were to deploy in open order and dig shelter-trenches for ourselves—though I can tell the reader that "shelter" is a poor word to use in such a connection. It seems we had to wait for artillery before making the attack on Navarin itself. The trench "Spandau," so Delpeuch told me, was being put into shape by the engineers and was already partially filled with troops who were coming up to our support. The same message had been carried to the other section. As we filed out of our pit, we saw them leaving theirs. In somewhat loose formation, we ran full tilt down the hill, and, at the assigned position, flung ourselves on the ground and began digging like mad. We had made the last stretch without losing a man.

The Ferme Navarin was two hundred metres from where we lay. From it came a heavy rifle and *mitrailleuse* fire, but we did not respond. We had something else to do. Every man had his shovel, and every man made the dirt fly. In what seemed half a minute we had formed a continuous parapet, twelve. to fourteen inches in height, and with our knapsacks placed to keep the dirt in position, we felt quite safe against infantry and machine-gun fire. Next, each man proceeded to dig his little individual niche in the ground, about a yard deep, twenty inches wide, and long enough to lie down in with comfort. Between each

1. Kriegs Kartoffel Brot.

114

two men there remained a partition wall of dirt, from ten to fifteen inches thick, the usefulness of which was immediately demonstrated by a shell which fell into Blondino's niche, blowing him to pieces without injuring either of his companions to the right or the left.

We were comfortable and able to take pot shots at the Germans and to indulge again in the old bench game of sticking a helmet on a bayonet, pushing it a little above the dirt, and thus coaxing the Germans into a shot and immediately responding with four or five rifles. I looked at my watch. It said 10.45—just an hour and a half since we had left our trenches and started on our charge; an hour and a half in which I had lived days and years.

I was pretty well tired out and would have given the world for a few hours' sleep. I called to Merrick to toss me Blondino's canteen. Mine was empty, and Blondino had left his behind when he departed with the 105-millimetre. Haeffle remarked that Blondino was always making a noise anyway.

The artillery fire died down gradually and only one German battery was still sweeping us now. Our long-range pieces thundered behind us, and we could hear shells "*swooshing*" overhead in a constant stream on their way to the German target. Our fire was evidently beating down the German artillery fire excepting the single battery which devoted its attention to us. The guns were hidden, and our artillery did not seem able to locate them. Our aeroplanes, long hovering overhead, began to swoop dangerously low. A swift Morane plane swept by at a height of two hundred metres over the pine forest where the German guns were hidden. We watched him as he returned safe to our lines.

Soon the order came down the line to deepen the trenches. It seemed we were to stay there until night.

The charge was over.

CHAPTER 5

Buried Alive!

Time passed vary slowly. I raised my arm to listen to my wristwatch, but couldn't hear it. Too many shells!

I knelt cautiously in my hole, and, looking over the edge, counted my section. There were but eighteen men. The Collettes, both corporals, were on the extreme left. Next came Capdeveille, Dowd, Zinn, Seeger, Scanlon, King, Soubiron, Dubois, Corporal Mettayer, Haeffle, Saint-Hilaire, Schneli, De Sumera, Corporal Denis, Bur-bek-kar, and Birchler. On my left, two paces in the rear of the section, were Neumayer, Corporal Fourrier, and Sergeant Fourrier. Both these were supernumeraries. The second sergeant was over with Section II. I began now to realize our losses. Fully two thirds of my section were killed or wounded.

I wanted information from Corporal Denis regarding the men of his squad. Throwing a lump of dirt at him to attract his attention, I motioned to him to roll over to the side of his hole and make a place for me. Then, with two quick jumps I landed alongside him. As I dropped we noticed spurts of dust rising from the dirt-pile in front of the hole and smiled. The Germans were too slow that time. Putting my lips to his ears, I shouted my questions and got my information.

This hole was quite large enough to accommodate both of us, so I decided to stay with him awhile. Corporal Denis still had bread and cheese and shared it with me. We lunched in comfort.

Having finished, we rolled cigarettes. I had no matches, and as he reached his cigarette to me to light mine, he jumped almost to his feet, rolled on his face, and with both hands clasped to his face, tried to rise, but couldn't. I've seen men who were knocked out in the squared ring do the same thing. With heads resting on the floor, they try to get up. They get up on their knees and seem to try to lift their heads,

116

but can't. Denis tugged and tugged, without avail. I knelt alongside him and forced his hands from his face. He was covered with blood spurting out of a three-inch gash running from the left eye down to the corner of the mouth. A steel splinter had entered there and passed under the left ear. He must stay in the trench until nightfall.

I reached for his emergency dressing and as I made the motion felt a blow in the right shoulder. As soon as I had got Denis tied up and quiet, I unbuttoned my coat and shirt and picked a rifle-ball out of my own shoulder. The wound was not at all serious and bled but little. I congratulated myself, but wondered why the ball did not penetrate; and then I caught sight of Denis's rifle lying over the parapet and showing a hole in the woodwork. The ball seemed to have passed through the magazine of the rifle, knocked out one cartridge, and then hit me.

When I was ready to return to my own hole, I rose a little too high and the Germans turned loose with a machine gun, but too high. I got back safely and lay down. It was getting very monotonous. To pass the time, I dug my hole deeper and larger, placing the loose dirt in front in a quarter-circle, until I felt perfectly safe against anything except a direct hit by a shell. There is but one chance in a thousand of that happening.

The day passed slowly and without mishap to my section. As night fell, one half of the section stayed on the alert four hours, while the other half slept. The second sergeant had returned and relieved me at twelve, mid- night. I pulled several handfuls of grass, and with that and two overcoats I had stripped from dead Germans during the night, I made a comfortable bed and lay down to sleep. The bank was not uncomfortable. I was very tired, and dozed off immediately.

Suddenly I awoke in darkness. Everything was still, and I could hear my watch ticking, but over every part of me there was an immense leaden weight. I tried to rise, and couldn't move. Something was holding me and choking me at the same time. There was no air to breathe. I set my muscles and tried to give a strong heave. As I drew in my breath, my mouth filled with dirt. I was buried alive!

It is curious what a man thinks about when he is in trouble. Into my mind shot memories of feats of strength performed. Why, I was the strongest man in the section. Surely I could lift myself out, I thought to myself, and my confidence began to return. I worked the dirt out of my mouth with the tip of my tongue and prepared myself mentally for the sudden heave that would free me. A quick inhalation, and my mouth filled again with dirt. I could not move a muscle under my skin. And then I seemed to be two people. The "I" who was thinking seemed to be at a distance from the body lying there.

My God! Am I going to die stretched out in a hole like this? I thought.

Through my mind flashed a picture of the way I had always hoped to die—the way I had a right to die: face to the enemy and running toward him. Why, that was part of a soldier's wages. I tried to shout for help, and more dirt entered my mouth! I could feel it gritting way down in my throat. My tongue was locked so I could not move it. I watched the whole picture. I was standing a little way off and could hear myself gurgle. My throat was rattling, and I said to myself, "That's the finish!" Then I grew calm. It wasn't hurting so much, and somehow or other I seemed to realize that a soldier had taken a soldier's chance and lost. It wasn't his fault. He had done the best he could. Then the pain all left me and the world went black. It was death.

Then somebody yelled, "Hell! He bit my finger." I could hear him.

"That's nothing," said a voice I knew as Collette's. "Get the dirt out of his mouth."

Again a finger entered my throat, and I coughed spasmodically.

Someone was working my arms backward, and my right shoulder hurt me. I struggled up, but sank to my knees and began coughing up dirt.

"Here," says Soubiron, "turn round and spit that dirt on your parapet. It all helps." The remark made me smile.

I was quite all right now, and Soubiron, Collette, Joe, and Marcel returned to their holes. The Red Cross men were picking something out of the hole made by a 250-millimetre, they told me. It was the remnant of Corporal and Sergeant Fourrier, who had their trench to my left. It seems that a ten-inch shell had entered the ground at the edge of my hole, exploded a depth of two metres, tearing the corporal and the sergeant to pieces, and kicking several cubic metres of dirt into and on top of me. Soubiron and the Collettes saw what had happened, and immediately started digging me out. They had been just in time. It wasn't long before my strength began to come back.

Two stretcher-bearers came up to carry me to the rear, but I declined their services. There was too much going on. I dug out the German overcoats, recovered some grass, and, bedding myself down in the crater made by the shell, began to feel quite safe again. Lightning never strikes twice in the same spot.

However, that wasn't much like the old-fashioned lightning. The enemy seemed to have picked upon my section. The shells were falling thicker and closer. Everybody was broad awake now, and all of us seemed to be waiting for a shell to drop into our holes. It was only a question of time before we should be wiped out. Haeffle called my attention to a little trench we all had noticed during the daytime, about forty metres in front of us. No fire had come from there, and it was evidently quite-abandoned.

I took Haeffle and Saint-Hilaire with me and quietly crawled over to the trench, round the end of it, and started to enter at about the middle.

Then all of a sudden a wild yell came out of the darkness in front of us.

"*Franzosen! Die Franzosen!*"

We couldn't see anything, nor they either. There might have been a regiment of us, or of them for that matter. I screeched out in German, "*Hände hoch!*" and jumped into the trench followed by my two companions. As we crouched in the bottom, I yelled again, "*Hände hoch oder wir schiessen!*"

The response was the familiar "*Kameraden! Kameraden!*" Haeffle gave an audible chuckle.

Calling again on my German, I ordered the men to step out of the trench with hands held high, and to march toward our line. I assured the poor devils we wouldn't hurt them. They thought there was a division of us, more or less, and I don't know how much confidence they put in my assurance. Anyhow, as they scrambled over the parapet, I counted six of them prisoners to the three of us. Haeffle and Saint-Hilaire escorted them back and also took word to the second sergeant to let the section crawl, one after the other, up this trench to where I was.

One by one the men came on, crawling in single file, and I put them to work, carefully and noiselessly reversing the parapet. This German trench was very deep, with niches cut into the bank at intervals of one metre, permitting the men to lie down comfortably.

It was then that I happened to feel of my belt One of the straps had been cut clean through and my wallet, which had held two hundred and sixty-five *francs*, had been neatly removed. Someone of my men, who had risked his life for mine with a self-devotion that could scarcely be surpassed, had felt that his need was greater than mine.

Whoever he was, I bear him no grudge. Poor chap, if he lived he needed the money—and that day he surely did me a good turn. Besides, he was a member of the Legion.

I placed sentries, took care to find a good place for myself, and was just dropping off to sleep as Haeffle and Saint-Hilaire returned and communicated to me the captain's compliments and the assurance of a "*citation*."

I composed myself to sleep and dropped off quite content.

CHAPTER 6

The German Trenches

It seemed but a few minutes when I was awakened by Collette and Marcel, who offered me a steaming cup of coffee, half a loaf of bread, and some Swiss cheese. This food had been brought from the rear while I was lying asleep. My appetite was splendid, and when Sergeant Malvoisin offered me a drink of rum in a canteen that he took off a dead German, I accepted gratefully. Just then the *agent de liaison* appeared, with the order to assemble the section, and in single file, second section at thirty-metre interval, to return the way we had come.

It was almost daylight and things were visible at two to three metres. The bombardment had died down and the quiet was hardly disturbed by occasional shots. Out captain marched ahead of the second section, swinging a cane and contentedly puffing on his pipe. Nearly everybody was smoking. As we marched along we noticed that new trenches had been dug during the night, from sixty to a hundred metres in the rear of the position we had held, and these trenches were filled by the Twenty-Ninth Chasseurs Regiment, which replaced us.

Very cunningly these trenches were arranged. They were deep and narrow, fully seven feet deep and barely a yard wide. At every favourable point, on every little rise in the ground, a salient had been constructed, projecting out from the main bench ten to fifteen metres, protected by heavy logs, corrugated steel sheets, and two to three feet of dirt. Each side of the salients bristled with machine guns. Any attack upon this position would be bound to fail, owing to the intense volume of fire that could be brought to bear upon the flanks of the enemy.

To make assurance doubly sure, the Engineer Corps had dug rows of cup-shaped bowls, two feet in diameter, two feet deep, leaving but a narrow wedge of dirt between each two; and in the centre of each bowl was placed a six-pointed twisted steel "porcupine." This instrument, no matter how placed, always presents a sharp point right at you. Five rows of these man-traps I counted, separated by a thin wall of dirt, not strong enough to maintain the weight of a man, so that anyone who attempted to rush past would be thrown against the "porcupine" and be spitted like a pigeon. As an additional precaution a mass of barbed wire lay in rolls, ready to be placed in front of this *ouvrage*, to make it safe against any surprise.

We marched along, talking and chatting, discussing this and that, without a care in the world. Every one hoped we were going to the rear to recuperate and enjoy a good square meal and a good night's rest. Seeger wanted a good wash, he said. He was rather dirty, and so was I. My *puttees* dangled in pieces round my calves. It seems I had torn them going through the German wire the day before. I told Haeffle to keep his eyes open for a good pair on some dead man. He said he would.

The company marched round the hill we descended so swiftly yesterday and, describing a semicircle, entered again the *Schützengraben Spandau* and marched back in the direction we had come from. The trench, however, presented a different appearance. The bad places had been repaired, the loose dirt had been shovelled out, and the dead had disappeared. On the east side of the trench an extremely high parapet had been built. In this parapet even loopholes appeared—rather runny-looking loopholes, I thought; and when I looked closer, I saw that they were framed in by boots! I reached my hand into several of them as we walked along, and touched the limbs of dead men. The engineer, it seems, in need of material, had placed the dead Germans on top of the ground, feet flush with the inside of the ditch, leaving from six to seven inches between two bodies, and laying another body crosswise on top of the two, spanning the gap between them. Then they had shovelled the dirt on top of them, thus killing two birds with one stone.

The discovery created a riot of excitement among the men. Curses intermingled with laughter came from ahead of us. Everybody was tickled by the ingenuity of our *génie*. "They are marvellous!" we thought. Dowd's face showed consternation, yet he could not help smiling. Little King was pale around the mouth, yet his lips were twisted in a grin. It was horribly amusing.

Every two hundred metres we passed groups of soldiers of the one Hundred and Seventieth Regiment on duty in the trench. The front line, they told us, was twelve hundred metres farther east, and this trench formed the second line for their regiment. We entered the third-line trench of the Germans, from which they ran yesterday to surrender, and continued marching in the same direction—always east. Here we had a chance to investigate the erstwhile German habitations.

Exactly forty paces apart doorways opened into the dirt bank, and from each of them fourteen steps descended at about forty-five degrees into a cellar-like room. The stairs were built of wood and the sides of the stairways and the chambers below were lined with one-inch pine boards. These domiciles must have been quite comfortable and safe, but now they were choked with bodies. As we continued our leisurely way, we met some of our trench-cleaners and they recited their experiences with gusto. The Germans, they told us, pointing down into the charnel-houses, refused to come and give up, and even fired at them when summoned to surrender.

"Then what did you do?" I asked.

"Very simple," answered one. "We stood on the top of the ground right above the door and hurled grenade after grenade through the doorway until all noise gradually ceased down below. Then we went to the next hole and did the same thing. It wasn't at all dangerous," he added, "and very effective."

We moved but slowly along the trench, and every once in a while there was a halt while some of the men investigated promising "prospects," where the holes packed with dead Germans held out some promise of loot. Owing to the order of march, the first company was the last one in line, and my section at the very end. The head of the column was the fourth company, then the third, the second; and then we. By the time my section came to any hole holding out hopes of souvenirs, there was nothing left for us. Yet I did find a German officer with a new pair of leg-bands, and, hastily unwinding them, I discarded my own and put on the new ones. As I bound them on I noticed the name on the tag—"*Hindenburg*." I suppose the name stands for quality with the Boches.

We left the trench and swung into another communication trench, going to the left, still in an easterly direction, straight on toward the Butte de Souain. That point we knew was still in the hands of the Germans, and very quickly they welcomed us. Shells came shrieking down—one hundred and five millimetres, one hundred and fifty, two hundred and ten, and two hundred and fifty. It's very easy to tell when you are close to them, even though you can't see a thing. When a big shell passes high, it sounds like white-hot piece of iron suddenly doused in cold water; but when it gets close, the *sw-i-ish* suddenly rises in a high *crescendo*, a shriek punctuated by a horrible roar. The uniformity of movement as the men ducked was beautiful!—and they all did it. One moment there was a line of gray helmets bobbing up and down the trenches as the line plodded on; and the next instant one could see only a line of black canvas close to the ground, as every man ducked and shifted his shoulder-sack over his neck. My sack had been blown to pieces when I was buried, and I felt uncomfortably handicapped with only my *musette* for protection against steel splinters.

About a mile from where we entered this *boyau*, we came to a temporary halt, then went on once more. The fourth company had come to a halt, and we squeezed past them as we marched along. Every man of them had his shovel out and had commenced digging a niche for himself. We passed the fourth company, then the third, then the second, and finally the first, second, and third sections of our own company. Just beyond, we ourselves came to a halt and, lining up one man per metre, started to organize the trench for defensive purposes. From the other side of a slight ridge, east of us, and about six hundred metres away, came the sound of machine guns. Between us and the ridge the Germans were executing a very lively *feu de barrage*, a screen of fire, prohibiting any idea of sending reinforcements over to the front line.

Attached for rations to my section were the commandant of the battalion, a captain, and three sergeants of the Ètat-Major. Two of the sergeants were at the trench telephone, and I could hear them report the news to the officers. "The Germans," they reported, "are penned in on three sides and are prevented from retreating by our artillery." Twice they had tried to pierce our line between them and the Butte de Souain, and twice they were driven back. Good news for us!

At 10 a.m. we seat three men from each section to the rear for the soup. At about eleven they reappeared with steaming marmites of soup, stew, and coffee, and buckets of wine. The food was very good, and disappeared to the last morsel.

After we had eaten, the captain granted me permission to walk along the ditch back to the fourth company. The trench being too crowded for comfort, I walked alongside to the second company, and searched for my friend Sergeant Velte. Finally I found him lying in a shell-hole, side by side with his adjutant and Sergeant Morin. All three were dead, torn to pieces by one shell shortly after we had passed them in the morning. At the third company they reported that Second Lieutenant Sweeny had been shot through the chest by a lost ball that morning. Hard luck for Sweeny![1] The poor devil had just been nominated *sous-lieutenant* at the request of the French Embassy in Washington, and when he was attached as supernumerary to the third company we all had hopes that he would have a chance to prove his merit.

In the fourth company also the losses were severe. The part of the trench occupied by the three companies was directly enfiladed by the German batteries on the Butte de Souain, and every little while a shell would fall square into the ditch and take toll from the occupants. Our company was fully a thousand metres nearer to these batteries, but the trenches we occupied presented a three-quarters face to the fire, and consequently were ever so much harder to hit. Even then, when I got back I found four men *hors de combat* in the fourth section. In my section two niches were demolished without any one being hit.

Time dragged slowly until four in the afternoon, when we had soup again. Many of the men built little fires and with the *Erbsenwurst* they had found on dead Germans prepared a very palatable soup by way of extra rations.

At four o'clock sentries were posted and everybody fell asleep. A steady rain was falling, and to keep dry we hooked one edge of our tent-sheet on the ground above the niche and placed dirt on top of it to hold. Then we pushed cartridges through the buttonholes of the tent, pinning them into the side of the trench and forming a good cover for the occupant of the hole. Thus we rested until the new day broke, bringing a clear sky and sunshine. This day, the 27th,—the third of the battle,—passed without mishap to my section. We spent our time eating and sleeping, mildly distracted by an intermittent bombardment.

---

1. Lieutenant Sweeny has returned to America.

CHAPTER 7

Butte de Souain

Another night spent in the same cramped quarters! We were getting weary of inactivity, and it was rather hard work to keep the men in the ditch. They sneaked off singly and in pairs, always heading back to the German dugouts, all bent on turning things upside down in the hope of finding some- thing of value to carry as a keepsake. Haeffle came back once with three automatic pistols but no cartridges. From another trip he returned with an officer's helmet, and the third time he brought triumphantly back a string three feet long of dried sausages. Haeffle always did have a healthy appetite and it transpired that on the way back he had eaten a dozen sausages, more or less. The dried meat had made him thirsty and he had drunk half a canteen of water on top of it. The result was, he swelled up like a poisoned pup, and for a time he was surely a sick man.

Zinn found two shiny German bayonets, a long thin one and one short and heavy, and swore he'd carry them for a year if he had to. Zinn hailed from Battle Creek and wanted to use them as brush-knives on camping trips in the Michigan woods; but alas, in the sequel they got too heavy and were dropped along the road. One man found a German pipe with a three-foot soft-rubber stem, which he intended sending to his brother as a souvenir. Man and pipe are buried on the slopes of the Butte de Souain. He died that same evening.

At the usual time, 4 p.m., we had soup, and immediately after came the order to get ready. Looking over the trench, we watched the fourth company form in the open back of the ditch and, marching past us in an oblique direction, disappear round a spur of wooded hill. The third company followed at four hundred metres' distance, then the second, and as they passed out of sight around the hill, we jumped out and, forming in line, sections at thirty-metre intervals, each company four

126

hundred metres in the rear of the one ahead, we followed, *arme à la bretelle.*

We were quite unobserved by the enemy, and marched the length of the hill for three fourths of a kilometre, keeping just below the crest. Above us sailed four big French battle-planes and some small aero scouts, on the lookout for enemy aircraft. For a while it seemed as if we should not be discovered, and the command was given to lie down. From where we lay we could observe clearly the ensuing scrap in the air, and it was worth watching. Several German planes had approached close to our lines, but were discovered by the swift-flying scouts. Immediately the little fellows returned with the news to the big planes, and we watched the monster biplanes mount to the combat. In a wide circle they swung, climbing, climbing higher and higher, and then headed in a beeline straight toward the German *tauben.*

As they approached within range of each other, we saw little clouds appear close to the German planes, some in front, some over them, and others behind; and then, after an interval, the report of the thirty-two-millimetre guns mounted on our battle-planes floated down to us, immediately followed like an echo by the crack of the bursting shell. Long before the Germans could get within effective range for their machine guns, they were peppered by our planes and ignominiously forced to beat a retreat. One "albatross" seemed to be hit. He staggered from one side to the other, then dipped forward, and, standing straight on his nose, dropped like a stone out of sight behind the forest crowning the hill.

Again we moved on, and shortly arrived at the southern spur of the hill. Here the company made a quarter turn to the left, and in the same formation began the ascent of the hill. The second company was just disappearing into the scrubby pine forest on top. We entered also, continued on to the top, and halted just below the crest. The captain called the officers and sergeants and, following him, we crawled on our stomachs up to the highest point and looked over.

Never shall I forget the panorama that spread before us! The four thin ranks of the second company seemed to stagger drunkenly through a sea of green fire and smoke. One moment gaps showed in the lines, only to be closed again as the rear files spurted. Undoubtedly they ran at top speed, but to us watchers they seemed to crawl, and at times almost to stop. Mixed in with the dark green of the grass covering the valley were rows of lighter colour, telling of the men who fell in that mad sprint. The continuous bombardment sounded like a giant drum beating an incredibly swift *rataplan*. Along the whole length of our bill this curtain of shells was dropping, levelling the forest and seemingly beating off the very face of the hill itself, clean down to the bottom of the valley. Owing to the proximity of our troops to the enemy's batteries we received hardly any support from our own big guns, and the *rôle* of the combatants was entirely reversed. The Germans had their innings then and full well they worked.

As the company descended into the valley the pace became slower, and at the beginning of the opposite slope they halted and faced back. Owing to the height of the Butte de Souain, they were safe, and they considered that it was their turn to act as spectators.

As our captain rose we followed and took our places in front of our sections. Again I impressed upon the minds of my men the importance of following in a straight line and as close behind one another as possible. "*Arme à la main!*" came the order, and slowly we moved to the crest and then immediately broke into a dog-trot. Instantly we were enveloped in flames and smoke. Hell kissed us welcome! Closely I watched the captain for the sign to increase our speed. I could have run a mile in record time, but he plugged steadily along, one, two, three, four, one, two, three, four, at a tempo of a hundred and eighty steps per minute, three to the second,—the regulation tempo. Inwardly I cursed his insistence upon having things *réglementaires*.

As I looked at the middle of his back, longing for him to hurry, I caught sight, on my right, of a shell exploding directly in the centre of the third section. Out of the tail of my eye I saw the upper part of Corporal Keraudy's body rise slowly into the air. The legs had disappeared, and with arms outstretched the trunk sank down upon the corpse of Varma, the Hindu, who had marched behind him. Instinctively, I almost stopped in my tracks—Keraudy was a friend of mine— but at the instant Corporal Mettayer, running behind me, bumped into my back, and shoved me again into life and action.

We were out of the woods then, and running down the bare slope of the hill. A puff of smoke, red-hot, smote me in the face, and at the same moment intense pain shot up my jaw. I did not think I was hit seriously, since I was able to run all right. Someone in the second section intoned the regimental march, "*Allons, Giron.*" Others took it up; and there in that scene of death and hell, this song portraying the lusts and vices of the *Légion Étrangère* became a very pecan of enthusiasm and courage.

Glancing to the right, I saw that we were getting too close to the second section, so I gave the signal for a left oblique. We bore away from them until once again at our thirty paces' distance. All at once my feet tangled up in something and I almost fell. It was long grass! Just then it seemed to grow upon my mind that we were down in the valley and out of range of the enemy. Then I glanced ahead, and not over a hundred metres away I saw the second company lying in the grass and watching us coming. As we neared, they shouted little pleasantries at us and congratulated us upon our speed.

"Why this unseemly haste?" one wants to know.

"You go to the devil!" answers Haeffle.

"*Merci, mon ami!*" retorts the first; "I have just come through his back kitchen."

Counting my section, I missed Dubois, Saint-Hilaire, and Schueli. Collette, Joe told me, was left on the hill.

The company had lost two sergeants, one corporal, and thirteen men, coming down that short stretch! We mustered but forty-five men, all told. One, Sergeant Terisien, had for four months commanded my section, the "American Section," but was transferred to the fourth section. From where we rested we could see him slowly descending the hill, bareheaded and with his right hand clasping his left shoulder. He had been severely wounded in the head, and his left arm was nearly torn off at the shoulder. Poor devil! He was a good comrade and a good soldier. Just before the war broke out he had finished his third enlistment in the Legion, and was in line for a discharge and pension when he died.

Looking up the awful slope we had just descended, we could see the bodies of our comrades, torn and mangled and again and again kicked up into the air by the shells. For two days and nights the hellish hail continued to beat upon that blood-soaked slope, until we finally captured the Butte de Souain and forced an entire regiment of Saxons to the left of the *butte* to capitulate.

Again we assembled in column of fours, and this time began the climb uphill. Just then I happened to think of the blow I had received under the jaw, and feeling of the spot, discovered a slight wound under my left jaw-bone. Handing my rifle to a man, I pressed slightly upon the sore spot and pulled a steel splinter out of the wound. A very thin, long sliver of steel it was, half the diameter of a dime and not more than a dime's thickness, but an inch and a half long. The metal was still hot to the touch. The scratch continued bleeding freely, and I did not bandage it at the time because I felt sure of needing my emergency dressing farther along.

Up near the crest of the hill we halted in an angle of the woods and lay down alongside the One Hundred and Seventy-second Regiment of infantry. They had made the attack in this direction on the twenty-fifth, but had been severely checked at this point. Infantry and machine-gun fire sounded very close, and lost bullets by the hundreds flicked through the branches overhead. The One Hundred and Seventy-second informed us that a battalion of the *Premier Étranger*, had entered the forest and was at that moment storming a position to our immediate left. Through the trees showed lights, brighter than day, cast from hundreds of German magnesium candles shot into the air.

Our officers were grouped with those of the other regiment, and after a very long conference they separated, each to his command. Our captain called the officers and subalterns of the company together, and in terse sentences explained to us our positions and the object of the coming assault. It was to be a purely local affair, it seemed, and the point was the clearing of the enemy from the hill we were on. On a map drawn to scale he pointed out the lay of the land.

It looked to me like a hard proposition. Imagine to yourself a toothbrush about a mile long and three eighths to one half mile wide. The back is formed by the summit of the hill, densely wooded, and the bristles are represented by four little ridges rising from the valley we had just crossed, each one crowned with strips of forest and uniting with the main ridges at right angles. Between each two lines of bristles are open spaces, from one hundred to one hundred and fifty metres wide. We of the second regiment were to deliver the assault parallel with the bristles and stretching from the crest down to the valley.

The other column was to make a demonstration from our left, running a general course at right angles to ours. The time set was eight o'clock at night.

Returning to our places, we informed the men of what they were in for. While we were talking we noticed a group of men come from the edge of the woods and form into company formation, and we could hear them answer to the roll-call. I went over and peered at them. On their coat-collars I saw the gilt "No. 1." It was the *Premier Étranger*.

As the roll-call proceeded, I wondered. The sergeant was deciphering with difficulty the names from his little *carnet*, and response after response was, "*Mort*." Once in a while the answer changed to, "*Mort sur le champ d'honneur*," or a brief "*Tombé*." There were twenty-two men

in line, not counting the sergeant and a corporal, who in rear of the line supported himself precariously on two rifles which served him as crutches. Two more groups appeared back of this one, and the same proceeding was repeated. As I stood near the second group I could just catch the responses of the survivors. "Duvivier": "*Présent.*"—"Selonti": "*Présent.*"—"Boismort": "*Tombé.*"—"Herkis": "*Mort.*"—"Carney": "*Mort.*"—"MacDonald" : "*Présent.*"—"Farnsworth": "*Mort sur le champ d'honneur,*" responded MacDonald. Several of the men I had known, Farnsworth among them. One officer, a second-lieutenant, commanded the remains of the battalion. Seven hundred and fifty men, he informed me, had gone in an hour ago, and less than two hundred came back.

"*Ah, mon ami,*" he told me, "*c'est bien chaud dans le bois.*"

Quietly they turned into column of fours and disappeared in the darkness. Their attack had failed. Owing to the protection afforded by the trees, our aerial scouts had failed to gather definite information of the defences constructed in the forest, and owing also to the same cause, our previous bombardment had been ineffective.

It was our job to remedy this. One battalion of the One Hundred and Seventy-Second was detached and placed in line with us, and at 8 p.m. sharp the commandant's whistle sounded, echoed by that of our captain.

Quietly we lined up at the edge of the forest, shoulder to shoulder, bayonets fixed. Quietly each corporal examined the rifles of his men, inspected the magazines, and saw that each chamber also held a cartridge with firing-pin down. As silently as possible we entered between the trees and carefully kept in touch with each other. It was dark in there, and we had moved along some little distance before our eyes were used to the blackness. As I picked my steps I prepared myself for the shock every man experiences at the first sound of a volley. Twice I fell down into shell-holes and cursed my clumsiness and that of some other fellows to my right. "The 'Dutch' must be asleep," I thought, "or else they beat it." Hopefully, the latter!

We were approaching the farther edge of the "toothbrush bristles," and breathlessly we halted at the edge of the little open space before us. About eighty metres across loomed the black line of another "row of bristles." I wondered.

The captain and second section to our right moved on and we kept in line, still slowly and cautiously, carefully putting one foot before the other. Suddenly from the darkness in front of us came four or five heavy reports like the noise of a shotgun, followed by a long *hiss*. Into the air streamed trails of sparks. Above our heads the hiss ended with a sharp crack, and everything stood revealed as though it were broad daylight At the first crash, the major, the captains—everybody, it seemed to me—yelled at the same time, "*En avant! Pas de charge!*"—and in full run, with fixed bayonets, we flew across the meadow. As we neared the woods we were met by solid sheets of steel balls. Roar upon roar came from the forest; the volleys came too fast, it shot into my mind, to be well aimed.

Then something hit me on the chest and I fell sprawling. Barbed wire! Everybody seemed to be on the ground at once, crawling, pushing, struggling through. My rifle was lost and I grasped my *parabellum*. It was a German weapon, German charges, German cartridges. This time the Germans were to get a taste of their own medicine, I thought. Lying on my back, I wormed through the wire, butting into the men in front of me and getting kicked in the head by Mettayer. As I crawled I could hear the *ping, ping*, of balls striking the wire, and the shrill moan as they glanced off and continued on their flight.

Putting out my hand, I felt loose dirt, and, lying flat, peered over the parapet. "Nobody home," I thought; and then I saw one of the Collette brothers in the trench come running toward me and ahead of him a burly Boche. I saw Joe make a one-handed lunge with the rifle, and saw the bayonet show fully a foot in front of the German's chest.

Re-forming, we advanced toward the farther fringe of the little forest. Halfway through the trees we lay down flat on our stomachs, rifle in right hand, and slowly, very slowly, wormed our way past the trees into the opening between us and our goal. Every man had left his knapsack in front or else hanging on the barbed wire, and we were in good shape for the work that lay ahead. But the sections and companies were inextricably mixed. On one side of me crawled a lieutenant of the One Hundred and Seventy-Second, and on the other a private I had never seen before. Still we were all in line, and when someone shouted, "*Feu de quatre cartouches!*" we fired four rounds, and after the command all crawled again a few paces nearer.

Several times we halted to fire, aiming at the sheets of flame spurting toward us. Over the Germans floated several parachute magnesium rockets, sent up by our own men, giving a vivid light and enabling us to shoot with fair accuracy. I think now that the German fire was too high. Anyway, I did not notice any one in my immediate vicinity getting hit. Though our progress was slow, we finally arrived at the main wire entanglement.

All corporals in the French army carry wire-nippers, and it was our corporal's business to open a way through the entanglement. Several men to my right, I could see one,—he looked like Mettayer,— lying flat on his back and, nippers in hand, snipping away at the wire overhead, while all of us behind kept up a murderous and constant fire at the enemy. Mingled with the roar of the rifles came the stuttering rattle of the machine guns, at moments drowned by the crash of hand-grenades. Our grenadiers had rather poor success with their missiles, however, most of them hitting trees in front of the trench. The lieutenant on my left had four grenades. I could see him plainly. With one in his hand, he crawled close to the wire, rolled on his back, rested an instant with arms extended, both hands grasping the grenade, then suddenly he doubled forward and back and sent the bomb flying over his head. For two—three seconds,—it seemed longer at the time,— we listened, and then came the roar of the explosion. He smiled and nodded to me, and again went through the same manoeuvre.

In the meantime I kept my *parabellum* going. I had nine magazines loaded with dum-dum balls I had taken from some dead Germans, and I distributed the balls impartially between three *créneaux* in front of me. On my right, men were surging through several breaks in the wire. Swiftly I rolled over and over toward the free lane and went through with a rush. The combat had degenerated into a hand-grenade affair. Our grenadiers crawled alongside the parapet and every so often tossed one of their missiles into it, while the others, shooting over their heads, potted the Germans as they ran to rear.

Suddenly the fusillade ceased, and with a crash, it seemed, silence and darkness descended upon us. The sudden cessation of the terrific rifle firing and of the constant rattling of the machine guns struck one like a blow. Sergeant Altoffer brought me some information about one of my men, and almost angrily. I asked him not to shout! "I'm not deaf yet," I assured him. "*Mon vieux*," he raged, "it's you who are shouting!"

I realized my fault and apologized and in return accepted a drink of wine from his canteen.

Finding the captain, we received the order to assemble the men and maintain the trench, and after much searching I found a few men of the section. The little scrap had cost the first section three more men. Soubiron, Dowd, and Zinn were wounded and sent to the rear. The One Hundred and Seventy-Second sent a patrol toward the farthest, the last, bristle of the toothbrush, with the order to reconnoitre thoroughly. An hour passed and they had not returned. Twenty minutes more went by and still no patrol. Rather curious, we thought. No rifle-shots had come from that direction nor any noise such as would be heard during a combat with the bayonet. The commandant's patience gave way and our captain received the order to send another patrol. He picked me and I chose King, Delpeuch, and Birchler. All three had automatics, King a *parabellum*, Delpeuch and Birchler, Brownings. They left their rifles, bayonets, and cartridge-boxes behind and in Indian file followed me at a full run in an oblique direction past the front of the company and, when halfway across the clearing, following my example, fell flat on the ground. We rested awhile to regain our wind and then began to slide on our stomachs at right angles to our first course.

We were extremely careful to remain silent. Every little branch and twig we moved carefully out of our way; with one hand extended we felt of the ground before us as we hitched ourselves along. So silent was our progress that several times I felt in doubt about any one being behind me and rested motionless until I felt the touch of Delpeuch's hand upon my foot. After what seemed twenty minutes, we again changed direction, this time straight toward the trees looming close to us. We arrived abreast of the first row of trees, and, lying still as death, listened for sounds of the enemy. All was absolutely quiet; only the branches rustled overhead in a light breeze. A long time we lay there but heard no sound. We began to feel somewhat creepy, and I was tempted to pull my pistol and let nine shots rip into the damnable stillness before us. However, I refrained, and, touching my neighbour, started crawling along the edge of the wood. Extreme care was necessary, owing to the numberless branches littering the ground. The sweat was rolling down my face.

Again we listened, and again we were baffled by that silence. I was angry then and started to crawl between the trees. A tiny sound of metal scratching upon metal and I almost sank into the ground! Quickly I felt reassured. It was my helmet touching a strand of barbed wire. Still no sound!

Boldly we rose and, standing behind trees, scanned the darkness. Over to our right we saw a glimmer of light, and, walking this time, putting one foot carefully before the other, we moved in that direction. When opposite we halted and—I swore. From the supposed trench of the enemy came the hoarse sound of an apparently drunken man singing the *chanson* "*La Riviera.*" Another voice offered a toast to "*La Légion.*"

Carelessly we made our way through the barbed wire, crawling under and stepping over the strands, jumped over a ditch and looked down into what seemed to be an underground palace. There they were—the six men of the One Hundred and Seventy-Second—three of them lying stiff and stark on benches, utterly drunk. Two were standing up disputing, and the singer sat in an armchair, holding a long-stemmed glass in his hand. Close by him were several unopened bottles of champagne upon the table. Many empty bottles littered the floor. The singer welcomed us with a shout and an open hand, to which we, however, did not immediately respond. The heartbreaking work while approaching this place rankled in our mind. The sergeant and corporal were too drunk to be of any help, while two of the men were crying, locked in each others' arms. Another was asleep, and our friend the singer absolutely refused to budge. So, after I had stowed two bottles inside my shirt (an example punctiliously followed by the others), we returned.

Leaving Birchler at the wire, I placed King in the middle of the clearing and Delpeuch near the edge of the wood held by us, and then reported. The captain passed the word along to the major, and on the instant we were ordered to fall in, and in column of two marched over to the abandoned trench, following the line marked by my men.

As we entered and disposed ourselves therein, I noticed all the officers, one after the other, disappear in the palace. Another patrol was sent out by our company, and, after ranging the country in our front, it returned safely. That night it happened to be the second company's turn to mount outposts, and we could see six groups of men, one corporal and five men in each, march out into the night, and somewhere, each in some favourable spot, they placed themselves at a distance of about one hundred metres away, to watch, while we slept the sleep of the just.

CHAPTER 8

Conclusion

Day came, and with it the *corvée* carrying hot coffee and bread. After breakfast another *corvée* was sent after picks and shovels, and the men were set to work remodelling the trench, shifting the parapet to the other side, building little outpost trenches and setting barbed wire. The latter job was done in a wonderfully short time, thanks to German thoroughness, since for the stakes to which the wire is tied the Boches had substituted soft iron rods, three quarters of an inch thick, twisted five times in the shape of a great corkscrew. This screw twisted into the ground exactly like a cork-puller into a cork. The straight part of the rod, being twisted upon itself down and up again every ten inches, formed six or seven small round loops in a height of about five feet.

Into these eyes the barbed wire was laid and solidly secured with short lengths of tying wire. First cutting the tying wire, we lifted the barbed wire out of the eyes, shoved a small stick through one and, turning the rod with the leverage of the stick, unscrewed it out of the ground and then reversing the process screwed it in again. The advantage of this rod is obvious. When a shell falls amidst this wire protection, the rods are bent and twisted, but unless broken off short they always support the wire, and even after a severe bombardment present a serious obstacle to the assaulters. In such cases wooden posts are blown to smithereens by the shells, and when broken off let the wire fall flat to the ground.

As I was walking up and down, watching the work, I noticed a large box, resting bottom up, in a deep hole opening from the trench. Dragging the box out and turning it over, I experienced a sudden flutter of the heart. There, before my astonished eyes, resting upon a little platform of boards, stood a neat little centrifugal pump painted green and on the base of it in raised iron letters I read the words "*Byron Jackson, San Francisco.*" I felt queer at the stomach for an instant. San Francisco! my home town! Before my eyes passed pictures of Market Street and the "Park." In fancy I was one of the Sunday crowd at the Cliff House. How could this pump have got so far from home? Many times I had passed the very place where it was made. How, I wonder, did the Boche get this pump? Before the war or through Holland? A California-built pump to clean water out of German trenches, in France! It was astonishing! With something like reverence I put the pump back again and, going to my place in the trench, dug out one of my bottles of champagne and stood treat to the crowd. Somehow, I felt almost happy.

As I continued my rounds I came upon a man sitting on the edge of the ditch surrounded by naked branches, busy cutting them into two-foot lengths and tying them together in the shape of a "cross." I asked him how many he was making, and he told me that he expected to work all day to supply the crosses needed along one battalion front. French and German were treated alike, he assured me. There was absolutely no difference in the size of the crosses.

As we worked, soup arrived, and when that was disposed of, the men rested for some hours. We were absolutely unmolested except by our officers.

But at one o'clock that night we were again assembled in marching rig, each man carrying an extra pick or shovel, and we marched along parallel with our trench to the summit of the *butte*. There we installed ourselves in the main line out of which the Germans were driven by the One Hundred and Seventy-Second. Things came easy now. There was no work of any kind to be done, and quickly we found some dry wood, built small fires and with the material found in dugouts brewed some really delightful beverages. Mine was a mixture of wine and water out of Haeffle's canteen, judiciously blended with chocolate.

The weather was delightful and we spent the afternoon lying in sunny spots, shifting once in a while out of the encroaching shade into the warm rays. We had no idea where the Germans were,—somewhere in front, of course, but just how far or how near mattered little to us. Anyway, the One Hundred and Seventy-Second were fully forty metres nearer to them than we were, and we could see and hear the first-line troops picking and shovelling their way into the ground.

Little King was, as usual, making the round of the company, trying to find someone to build a fire and get water if he, King, would furnish the chocolate. He found no takers and soon he laid himself down, muttering about the laziness of the outfit.

Just as we were dozing deliriously, an agonized yell brought every soldier to his feet. Rushing toward the cry, I found a man sitting on the ground, holding his leg below the knee with both hands and moaning as he rocked back and forth. "*Je suis blessé! Je suis blessé!*" Brushing his hands aside I examined his limb. There was no blood. I took off the leg-band, rolled up his trousers, and discovered no sign of a wound. I asked the man again where the wound was, and he passed his hand over a small red spot on his shin. Just then another man picked up a small piece of shell, and then the explanation dawned upon me. The Germans were shooting at our planes straight above us; a bit of shell had come down and hit our sleeper on the shin-bone. Amid a gale of laughter he limped away to a more sympathetic audience. Several more pieces of iron fell near us. Some fragments were no joking matter, being the entire rear end of three-inch shells weighing, I should think, fully seven pounds.

At 4 p.m. the soup *corvée* arrived. Besides the usual soup we had roast mutton, one small slice per man, and a mixture of white beans, rice, and string beans. There was coffee, and one cup of wine per man, and, best of all, tobacco. As we munched our food our attention was attracted to the sky above by an intense cannonade directed against several of our aeroplanes sailing east. As we looked, more and more of our war-birds appeared. Whipping out my glasses, I counted fifty-two machines. Another man counted sixty. Haeffle had it a hundred. The official report next day stated fifty-nine. They were flying very high and in very open formation, winging due east. The shells were breaking ahead of them and between them. The heaven was studded with hundreds upon hundreds of beautiful little round grayish clouds, each one the nimbus of a bursting shell. With my prismatics glued to my eyes I watched closely for one falling bird. Though it seemed incredible at the moment, not one faltered or turned back. Due east they steered, into the red painted sky. For several minutes after they had sailed out of my sight I could still hear the roar of the guns. Only one machine, the official report said, was shot down, and that one fell on the return trip.

Just before night fell, we all set to work cutting pine branches, and with the tips prepared soft beds for ourselves. Sentries were placed, one man per section, and we laid ourselves down to sleep. The night passed quietly; again the day started with the usual hot coffee and bread. Soup and stew at 10 a.m., and the same again at 4 p.m. One more quiet night and again the following day. We were becoming somewhat restless with the monotony but were cheered by the captain. That night, he told us, we should return to Suippes and there we should re-form the regiment and rest. The programme sounded good, but I felt very doubtful, so many times we had heard the same tale and so many times we had been disappointed. Each day the *corvées* had brought the same news from the kitchen.

At least twenty times different telephonists and *agents de liaison* had brought the familiar story. The soup *corvées* assured us that the drivers of the rolling kitchens had orders to hitch up and pull out toward Souain and Suippes. The telephonists had listened to the order transmitted over the wires. The *agents de liaison* had overheard the commandant telling other officers that he had received marching orders and, "*Ma foi!* each time each one was wrong!" So after all, I was not much disappointed when the order came to unmake the sacks.

We stayed that night and all that day, and when the order to march the following evening came, all of us were surprised, including the captain. I was with the One Hundred and Seventy-Second at the time, having some fun with a little Belgian. I had come upon him in the dark and had watched him in growing wonder at his actions. There the little fellow was, stamping up and down, every so often stopping, shaking clenched fists in the air, and spouting curses. I asked him what was the matter. "*Rien, mon sergent,*" he replied. "*Je m'excite.*" "*Pourquoi?*" I demanded. "Ah," he told me, "look,"—pointing out toward the German line,—"out there lies my friend, dead, with three pounds of my chocolate in his *musette*, and when I'm good and mad, I'm going out to get it!" I hope he got it!

That night at seven o'clock we left the hill, marched through Souain four miles to Suippes and sixteen miles farther on, at Saint-Hilaire, we camped. A total of twenty-six miles.

At Suippes the regiment passed in parade march before some officer of the *État-Major,* and we were counted:—eight hundred and fifty-two in the entire regiment, out of thirty-two hundred who entered the attack on the 25th of September.

141

LEONAUR

ALSO FROM LEONAUR
AVAILABLE IN SOFTCOVER OR HARDCOVER WITH DUST JACKET

FARAWAY CAMPAIGN *by F. James*—Experiences of an Indian Army Cavalry Officer in Persia & Russia During the Great War.

REVOLT IN THE DESERT *by T. E. Lawrence*—An account of the experiences of one remarkable British officer's war from his own perspective.

MACHINE-GUN SQUADRON *by A. M. G.*—The 20th Machine Gunners from British Yeomanry Regiments in the Middle East Campaign of the First World War.

A GUNNER'S CRUSADE *by Antony Bluett*—The Campaign in the Desert, Palestine & Syria as Experienced by the Honourable Artillery Company During the Great War .

DESPATCH RIDER *by W. H. L. Watson*—The Experiences of a British Army Motorcycle Despatch Rider During the Opening Battles of the Great War in Europe.

TIGERS ALONG THE TIGRIS *by E. J. Thompson*—The Leicestershire Regiment in Mesopotamia During the First World War.

HEARTS & DRAGONS *by Charles R. M. F. Crutwell*—The 4th Royal Berkshire Regiment in France and Italy During the Great War, 1914-1918.

INFANTRY BRIGADE: 1914 *by John Ward*—The Diary of a Commander of the 15th Infantry Brigade, 5th Division, British Army, During the Retreat from Mons.

DOING OUR 'BIT' *by Ian Hay*—Two Classic Accounts of the Men of Kitchener's 'New Army' During the Great War including *The First 100,000* & *All In It*.

AN EYE IN THE STORM *by Arthur Ruhl*—An American War Correspondent's Experiences of the First World War from the Western Front to Gallipoli-and Beyond.

STAND & FALL *by Joe Cassells*—With the Middlesex Regiment Against the Bolsheviks 1918-19.

RIFLEMAN MACGILL'S WAR *by Patrick MacGill*—A Soldier of the London Irish During the Great War in Europe including *The Amateur Army*, *The Red Horizon* & *The Great Push*.

WITH THE GUNS *by C. A. Rose & Hugh Dalton*—Two First Hand Accounts of British Gunners at War in Europe During World War 1- Three Years in France with the Guns and With the British Guns in Italy.

THE BUSH WAR DOCTOR *by Robert V. Dolbey*—The Experiences of a British Army Doctor During the East African Campaign of the First World War.

www.ingramcontent.com/pod-product-compliance
Lightning Source LLC
Chambersburg PA
CBHW021009090426
42738CB00007B/712